The Yorkshire Three Peaks Challenge

with

Paul Shorrock

DISCOVERY WALKING GUIDES LTD

The Yorkshire Three Peaks Challenge
First Edition - July 2010
Second Edition - May 2013

Copyright © 2010, 2013

Published by
Discovery Walking Guides Ltd
10 Tennyson Close, Northampton NN5 7HJ, England

Mapping supplied by **Global Mapping Limited** (www.globalmapping.com)

This product includes mapping data licensed from **Ordnance Survey®** with the permission of the Controller of Her Majesty's Stationery Office. © Crown Copyright 2005. All rights reserved.

Licence Number 40044851

Photographs
The majority of the photographs in this book were taken by the author; others are reproduced here with the kind permission of John Bamber and Les Staves.

Front Cover Photographs

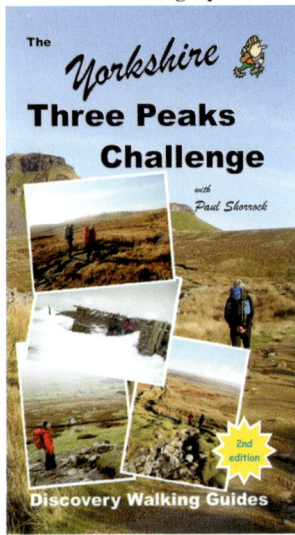

Background image: the approach from Brackenbottom (Walks 2, 4, 7).

Other images from the top:

- the approach to Whernside from Force Gill Ridge Walk 2),

- Pen y Ghent summit shelter (walks 1, 4, 7),

- the descent towards The Hill Inn from Whernside above Bruntscar (Walk 5),

- heading west towards Whernside summit ridge (Walk

ISBN 9781904946915
Text and photographs* © Paul Shorrock

All rights reserved. No part of this publication may be reproduced, stored in a retrieval system or transmitted in any form or by any means, electronic, mechanical, photocopying, recording or otherwise, without the prior written permission of the publishers.

The author and publishers have tried to ensure that the information and maps in this publication are as accurate as possible. However, we accept no responsibility for any loss, injury or inconvenience sustained by anyone using this book.

The Yorkshire Three Peaks Challenge

CONTENTS

Contents	3
The Author	5
Acknowledgements	5
Friends Reunited	6
Diary of a Project	9
Introduction	13
Geology and Landscape	14
Natural History	16
Human Influence	16
First Things First	20
Clothing and Equipment	20
Navigation	23
If Things Start to Go Wrong	24
Preparation	27
Getting Fit	27
Planning - the Strategy	28
The Day of the Challenge - Tactics	29
Tips for Success	30
Walk Location Map	32
Symbols Rating Guide & Notes on OS Mapping	33
Using GPS on the Yorkshire Three Peaks Challenge	34
THE WALKS	

MAKING A START - THREE PEAKS, ONE AT A TIME   36

1. **Peny Ghent from Horton in Ribblesdale**   37
   4 walker, 3 hour 15 mins, 5.8 miles/9.3km, ascents & descents 488 metres, 4 refreshments (circular)

2. **Whernside from Ribblehead**   42
   4 walker, 4 hours, 7.8 miles/12.6km, ascents & descents 478 metres, 4 refreshments (circular)

3. **Ingleborough from the Hill Inn**   47
   4 walker, 4 hours, 7.9 miles/12.8km, ascents & descents 513 metres, 4 refreshments (circular)

THE MISSING LINKS - FILLING IN THE GAPS   52

4   Horton in Ribblesdale, Pen y Ghent, Ribblehead   53
5 walker, 5½ hours, 10.25 miles/16.5km, ascents 647 metres, descents 587 metres, 4 refreshments (linear)

5   Ribblehead, Whernside, Hill Inn, Ribblehead   59
4 walker, 4 hours, 7.8 miles/12.5km, ascents & descents 528 metres, 4 refreshments (circular)

6   Ribblehead, Hill Inn, Ingleborough, Horton in Ribblesdale   64
5 walker, 4¼ hours, 9.5 miles/15.4km, ascents 492, metres, descents 564 metres, 4 refreshments (linear)

THE THREE PEAKS CHALLENGE

7   The Big Day!   70
5+ walker, 11¾ hours, 21.75 miles/35km, ascents & descents 1570 metres (circular)

After the Three Peaks Challenge   82

Some Final Thoughts   84

GPS Waypoints and Co-ordinates   86

Accommodation   88

Other Useful Information   90

Glossary   92

Place Names Index   94

THE AUTHOR

Paul Shorrock began hill walking in his late teens, and is still at it. Along the way he picked up scrambling, rock climbing, fell running and caving in roughly that order, and is now in the process of giving them up in reverse order.

Over the past forty years Paul has been a member of a Lake District mountain rescue team for seventeen years and a search dog handler with the Search and Rescue Dogs Association for five years. In 1983 he qualified for the award of the Mountain Leaders Certificate (Summer).

Paul finished full time work in 2005, and now runs his own web-based business, offering guided hill walks in the Yorkshire Dales, Lake District, North Wales and Scotland and also navigation and hillcraft training. He is a course provider and assessor for the National Navigation Award Scheme (NNAS), and a member of the Mountain Leader Training Association (MLTA) and the British Mountaineering Council (BMC).

As well as writing for Discovery Walking Guides, Paul also writes for the walkingworld.com website. He also walks for fun, usually with his wife, Chris.

ACKNOWLEDGEMENTS

Thanks are due to Ros and David of Discovery Walking Guides for their patience, advice and encouragement during the Y3P project, and to Chris and Dave Stewart of Walking World for setting me off in the first place.

Thanks also go to Les Staves who provided some excellent photographs, and John Bamber for his photographs, advice, company on some of the walks and his unfailing sense of humour.

Finally thanks go to my long-suffering wife Chris who, as well as accompanying me on most of my walks, also helped enormously on this project with proof reading, style issues and encouragement.

Any mistakes or errors are mine alone.

FRIENDS REUNITED

Parking the car at **Ribblehead**, I went into my tour guide mode. "This is one of the best bits of the Yorkshire Dales. From here you can see the Three Peaks of Ingleborough, Whernside and Pen y Ghent". Kim and Tricia seemed reasonably impressed with the Dales scenery, so I carried on. "There's a well known challenge walk linking all three – it's about twenty four miles". "I'd quite like to do that", said Kim, and I knew that he meant it.

I've known Kim for over thirty years. We were on the same officer-training course in the Royal Marine Commandos, he not long out of sixth form at the time, me six years older and a lance corporal with 1½ years service behind me. Like many service mates, we see each other about every ten or fifteen years, and it seems like it's been ten or fifteen days. Apart from the changing hairstyles and wrinkles, that is.

The Three Peaks are even older friends. When I was nineteen, four of us did the Three Peaks walk for the Duke of Edinburgh's Award. We took three days, and rucksacks weighing 15 kgs (over 30 lbs). Living in the hills for a couple of days or more cements a bond, both with friends and the hills themselves.

The next time I did the challenge walk was fifteen years later. I went lightweight, in fell running gear, with just the dog for company. I have two vivid memories of that circuit. The first is ploughing knee-deep into a bog on the final stretch between **Pen y Ghent** and **Ribblehead**. Every time I tried to lift one leg out, I got cramp in the other leg. After hopping from leg to leg for about a minute, I got out without having to swim it!

The second memory of the day was arriving back at the tent at **Ribblehead**, my start point. The dog, who had already covered twice the distance that I had, came up to me with a ball, wanting a game. Of course, being a Border Collie he didn't understand the word 'tired'. I got round in a little under six hours, and could probably have knocked off another hour if I hadn't become dehydrated on the way round.

Back to more recent times. It was over a year after our conversation in the car at **Ribblehead** that I received an email from Kim. He had a window of opportunity between jobs, and fancied doing the Three Peaks. I would have preferred a bigger window, with an option of several days to take advantage of the best weather conditions, but Kim had only three days, one to travel to Yorkshire, one for the walk, and one to get home.

Start of the day - Whernside from Ribblehead

An early start on 13th August 2009 had us ready for action at **Ribblehead** before eight o'clock in the morning, having already cached water at **Horton in Ribblesdale** and **Chapel le Dale**, near the **Hill Inn**.

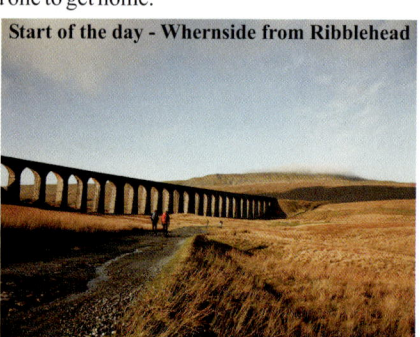

Ingleborough - the half-way point

There was cap of cloud on **Ingleborough**, but otherwise the sky was clear, with a hint of cool in the morning air. So, at least the weather gods were smiling on us.

We set off for **Whernside**, following the route that the serious fell runners take, from near **Winterscales** and straight up the side of the fell (Walk 5 in this guide). The route can only be described as steep, though at the time I could think of several other words, most of them unrepeatable.

Our last peak - Pen y Ghent crags

From the top we could see for miles, but there was no time to hang about. **Ingleborough** was beckoning across the dale.

An easy descent took us to the road near the **Hill Inn**, and our first water cache. We got through a litre each, both with drinking and refilling bottles. There was no way I was going to get dehydrated this time. I found the steady walk across **Southerscales** and the moor beyond quite relaxing, though Kim confessed afterwards that this was the low point for him. He wasn't showing it the time, though, and several times I suggested cutting the pace a bit, so as not to burn ourselves out.

It was a bit cool on the summit of **Ingleborough**, and I put on a micro-fleece top after the summit photo. We kept up a good pace through **Sulber Nick**. Just beyond there we took ten minutes out to help a couple of women with a map-reading problem, then we pressed on to **Horton in Ribblesdale** for our next water stop.

Pen y Ghent was the last hill for the day - I like to start the Challenge route at **Ribblehead** so I can finish with **Pen y Ghent**, my favourite of the three. We took the classic route by **Brackenbottom** and the south ridge. Again, we didn't linger, and set off from the summit heading towards our start point just below **Whernside** - it looked a long way off.

We followed the traditional route over **Todber Moss** and **Red Moss**. In this case, "moss" translates as "bog", and it was somewhere along this section that I'd had my knee-deep bog experience all those years earlier. It wasn't as bad this time, as the weather had been dry for a while, but constant criss-crossing to avoid the really wet bits had me thinking that there must be a better route, and that if I ever came this way again, I would not come this way again, if you see my meaning.

The bog behind us, all that remained was some good old Royal Marine 'yomping' along paths, tracks and roads. We arrived back at **Ribblehead** in good style, in less than nine hours. We hadn't tried to break any records, but we would probably have done it in less than eight hours had I not been so cautious about starting too quickly and burning out.

The only times that we stopped walking were on the three summits, the two water stops and the map reading workshop at **Sulber**. Food was taken on the move. I had a bag of nuts with dried fruit, and a couple of bars of chocolate. Kim survived on flapjack and the couple of bars of chocolate he blagged off me.

On the day of the walk I was four days short of my 59th birthday, and hill-walking about three or four times a month. Kim, still a major in the Royal Marines, keeps himself in shape, but he has demanding work schedules that take up much of his time, so he doesn't get out on the hills at all. Mind you, he is six years younger than me! Neither of us trained for the walk beforehand. Neither did we consider at any time that we wouldn't finish.

What we wanted was exactly what we got. A good walk out, in good company, with good chat along the way.

And if anyone reading this is wondering, "Could I do that?" the answer is a definite, "Yes". So, read on, do the preparation, get fit, do the practice walks, and finally have a great day walking the Yorkshire Three Peaks Challenge.

DIARY OF A PROJECT

As Kim and I sat down to our post Three Peaks drinks, I little suspected that three months later I would be speaking to David and Ros at Discovery Walking Guides about writing a guidebook for the walk. It did occur to me at the time that there could be difficulties in starting such a project in winter, such as the poor light for photographs and the weight of extra clothing and gear to be carried.

I quite like solo walking, but it became obvious that a little help on the project might not go amiss. Friends were canvassed for photos, with some stunning material coming from Les Staves. In addition I co-opted two people onto the project, both of whom are old enough to know better. Chris, my wife, is my usual walking companion, and she brings a more down to earth view to the party. The phrase, "Do you really expect people to walk *there*?" can sometimes modify my dafter ideas. She is also my best critic when it comes to writing up the routes.

John Bamber, on the other hand, is as barmy as me, perhaps more so. I met John in my late teens, and our first project together was canoeing from the Isle of Man to Blackpool (don't ask!). We subsequently shared the experience of sailing a 27-foot open boat around Morecambe Bay and the Irish Sea and we both started potholing at around the same time. When I gave up the underground to concentrate on the mountains, John carried on caving. He's since discovered the joys of high places, and is now an experienced alpine mountaineer as well as having substantial experience of working in the Arctic. Most importantly for this project, he's a far better photographer than I am.

So, the team being assembled, the project went something like this:-

Walking through mud ..

18 November, Walk 3, Ingleborough

For various reasons of logistics and convenience, I did this walk alone. The day was foul, with persistent rain and strong winds, but at least it gave me a chance to field test some Goretex salopettes that hadn't been used much until then.

A delayed start guaranteed that I would be finishing in the dark, but it was an enjoyable walk out. Towards the end I met two walkers doing the Challenge route. Unfortunately for them this was at **Great Douk Cave**, which was on my intended route, but not on theirs! Final score at the end of the day was Goretex - 2, rain - nil.

26 November

The forecast was dire, with strong winds and hail. Chris and I had a photographic day and managed to expand our stock of photos of some of the

.. and sometimes snow ..

lower locations. We did no walking but still managed to get wet and cold.

3 December, Walk 5, Whernside
John and I did this one. The weather forecast was set to be worse than the previous two trips, but apart from snow above 600 metres it wasn't all that bad, with the sun breaking out towards the end of the day. On the way round we carried out some interesting in-depth research inside **The Hill Inn** - cider for me, bitter for John.

5 December, Walk 1, Pen y Ghent
Chris and I set out hopefully, lulled into a false sense of security by a fairly benign weather forecast. It was cool and misty up to the summit, where things took a sudden change, and we were reminded that **Pen y Ghent** means "Hill of the Winds". The mist disappeared, but the wind was what is known in Yorkshire as "a lazy wind"; it can't be bothered going round you, so it goes straight through you! The snow of the previous few days was frozen on the descent route, requiring extra care. The pub was warm, though.

10 December, Walk 2
At last, a sunny day, with blue skies. Chris, John and I had a great day, as did several other walkers who had taken the opportunity of a fair day's walking. If only it was like this every time.

14 December
On our way home from a music session the previous evening, Chris and I dropped in at Horton, and researched some of the link route from **Pen y Ghent** to **Ribblehead** (Walk 4), the idea being to find an alternative to the morass of **Todber Moss** that didn't require too much of a detour. We managed to include a visit to **Hull Pot**, including some photographs.

The festivities of Christmas and New Year required our undivided attention, so there was a temporary halt to researching and writing. There was one trip out though:-

30 December
The intention had been to meet at the **Station Inn** at **Ribblehead** for a music session and a photo opportunity of a steam train crossing **Ribblehead Viaduct**. John's wife wasn't well, so the trip was cancelled, but John went on a solo trip for the photo. After battling for an hour in near blizzard conditions he arrived at the bridge next to **Blea Moor** tunnel. He bent down to get his cameras out of his rucksack, and heard the 'whoosh' of the train passing below him in the cutting, possibly the first time a train has ever been early in Britain! In John's words, "It made no difference, because you couldn't see anything for the horizontal snow".

Early January saw a return to the writing, with Walks 2 and 5 being finished, together with much of the background stuff.

7 January

Solo ski ascent **Pen y Ghent**. A totally self indulgent day, starting from **Horton** and skiing up **Horton Lane** then up the usual descent route. Unstable powder snow on the final bit, plus adjacent avalanche debris, suggested an earlier than planned return to the valley.

Over the next couple of weeks, more of the additional sections were completed in rough, then polished up before sending to Ros at Discovery Walking Guides for layout.

27 January

Walk 4 research with John. Yet another foray to sort out the best route to avoid the morass of **Todber Moss**.

We tried a detour down to **Sell Gill Holes**, but this was less than satisfactory; a gate was padlocked, and had to be climbed, and the route itself was far from straightforward to follow. We also had mist all day, which didn't help with the route finding, but this is a common feature of walking in the Yorkshire Dales. An easier, more obvious route, was needed.

.. with John trying to take photos in the mist ..

We had intended to walk a linear route from my car at **Horton** to John's car at **Ribblehead**. Halfway through the walk John started laughing, before telling me that his car keys were in my car back at Horton!

10 February

Walk 4 completed at last. The need to find a route avoiding the bog had made this section the biggest challenge. Unfortunately, bad weather had made it difficult to get out on the ground to finish the job, but at last a reasonably settled day came along. I was the only one available, so I went out solo. The day started with brilliant sunshine, but as usual the "Hill of the Winds" was well named. The wind was from the east, and as cold as an east wind can be, so I didn't linger on the summit of **Pen y Ghent**.

.. all in all, the research was quite demanding.

The usual descent route was banked up with steep hard snow, running down to boulders and scree - not a good place to slip! Care and cunning got me across the obstacle, but an ice axe would have been useful. On the way down to **Horton Lane** I was enveloped in a heavy snow storm, the first of several that day. The earlier research paid off, and the route to avoid **Todber Moss** was

An added distraction ..

finally recorded on GPS. The day finished with the long plod to **Ribblehead**, made longer by the winter-weight rucksack.

More heavy snow during the rest of February and early March made a trip to **Ingleborough** for Walk 6 pointless, as photography was out of the question. Instead I spent the time usefully, finishing off more of the background sections, and trawling through old photographs for extra material. There was also an extra distraction on the scene at this time with a new arrival at home, a boisterous Border Collie pup called Meg.

There was still a good bit of snow lying on **Ingleborough** in mid March, so I decided to abandon Yorkshire to have some fun in Wales. A day on Snowdon with ice axe and crampons made up for the delays with the Y3P project. The next day the weather forecast for Yorkshire indicated one day of fair weather coming, and the **Ingleborough** webcam showed that most of the snow had gone, so plans were hurriedly brought forward.

23 March

On 23 March I set off finally to complete Walk 6, and with it the whole project. It was two days after the first day of spring, and although there was a chill in the air there was also a change from the short, wintry days to the first signs of the returning summer.

.. Meg on the hills.

Perhaps the best sign as far as I was concerned, was that I was finally carrying my summer weight rucksack for the first time since I had started the project the previous November; it felt as light as a feather compared with the winter gear I had been carrying.

The walk went well, leaving only the loose ends to be tied. Back at home the GPS tracks for the main Challenge route were merged from the research walks, and the final sections of the background sections finished off, interspaced with walks and training sessions for Meg.

Finishing the project brought the same satisfaction that walkers feel on completion of the Challenge walk, together with a familiarity with the area that I hadn't had before.

For me, the trips to the Three Peaks area of Yorkshire were finished for the time being, but with the possibility of new projects on the horizon. One thing was certain; I had a great time with the project! Now it's your turn to try the Yorkshire Three Peaks Challenge.

INTRODUCTION

The Three Peaks of the Yorkshire Dales provide some of the finest walking in Britain. With a combination of high peaks and stunning scenery, the area is rightly popular with outdoor types from leisure walkers to super-fit fell runners. It always seems to follow that when you have a mix of high places and human beings, sooner or later someone will come up with an idea of a challenge of some kind. With the Three Peaks of **Pen y Ghent**, **Whernside** and **Ingleborough** the solution was simple - do them all in one walk!

The Pen y Ghent Café - home of the Three Peaks Challenge

The Yorkshire Three Peaks Challenge was already popular as a challenge walk long before the better-known National Three Peaks Challenge of Snowdon, Scafell Pike and Ben Nevis was even thought of. However, the idea of a recognised Yorkshire Three Peaks Challenge really took off after Peter and Joyce Bayes took over the **Pen y Ghent Café** in **Horton in Ribblesdale**, and subsequently created the "Three Peaks Club". Membership requirements were quite simple - book in and out at the café, and complete the circuit in 12 hours or less.

Walkers at the shelter, Ingleborough

The Yorkshire Three Peaks Challenge, as it's now known so as to avoid confusion with the National Challenge, remains popular. It's a great day out in magnificent surroundings - and what's more, it's within the ability of most walkers.

Previous walking experience is always an advantage, but each year the challenge is completed by people who hadn't previously looked at a hill, never mind walked up one, or up three hills in this case. Each year, however, there are those who fail to make it. This might be due to lack of fitness, carrying the wrong gear, errors in navigation (getting lost), not knowing what is involved or just having bitten off too much.

This guide is written to improve your chance of succeeding in the Challenge, and what's more important, enjoying your big day. To do this a simple method has been used; the routes in this book start with ascents of the Three Peaks, though tackling them one at a time, and following classic routes. In the next section we take on slightly longer routes that include the Peaks but also the bits linking the three different legs of the Challenge, again doing one at a time.

Finally, we take on the Challenge itself.

This obviously means that some sections of the route are repeated. This is intended to give walkers a good knowledge of the route by prior reconnaissance. It will also be useful in developing hill fitness for those who don't walk regularly, and will give an idea of how to deal with each section. The book will be equally useful for the experienced walker who is fit, has some knowledge of the area, and who only wants an accurate route description for the Challenge route.

But before we start walking the Challenge, it's interesting to find out a bit more about the dales and peaks.

GEOLOGY AND LANDSCAPE

The Three Peaks area of North Yorkshire has one of the most distinctive landscapes in Britain. The flat-topped peaks, white limestone escarpments and streams disappearing underground are instantly recognisable and quite unique. The peaks, although not the highest in Britain at about 700 metres (2300 ft), have beauty and drama. For many, however, the real beauty is in the valleys, the "Dales" that give the area its name.

The dominant rock is limestone, laid down over 300 million years ago. And it does dominate, forming a sweeping landscape of short-turfed green pastures and outcrops of white rock, with the distinctive shapes of the Three Peaks of **Ingleborough**, **Pen y Ghent** and **Whernside** rising above.

Limestone is a sedimentary rock composed of calcium deposits from the shells of marine creatures, laid down in what was a shallow tropical sea. Successive layers of these sediments were compressed into hard rock that hardly erodes at all by normal water action. However, when rain falls through the air it absorbs carbon dioxide and becomes acidic. This dissolves the limestone, helping to form the unique and dramatic landscape we see today.

Limestone pavement, looking towards Ingleborough

The most immediately obvious limestone features in the Dales are *Limestone Pavements* formed when glaciers scraped the already flat limestone layers, leaving a smooth surface. Acid rainwater seeped into cracks and joints, eventually forming blocks of rock known as *clints* separated by crevices known as *grikes*.

The water also seeped underground, travelling through fissures and seams until eventually emerging as a spring or *resurgence*.

Over many thousands of years the drainage routes have extended to create a labyrinth of passages, the horizontal ones creating caves, and the vertical ones forming *potholes*. *Potholes* are often huge and open to the surface, such as

Cave and stream resurgence, Ribblehead

Gaping Gill on the southern slopes of **Ingleborough**, where the shaft drops for 105 metres (360 ft) into the Main Chamber, one of the largest cave chambers in Britain, and big enough to contain York Minster.

Hull Pot, near Pen y Ghent

Surface potholes are usually formed by water drainage, forming a *sinkhole*, or *swallow hole*. Similar and related features are *shakeholes*, which are depressions in the ground, again caused by water drainage. Many of these are small craters no more than a metre deep, but occasionally much larger ones can be found, such as **Braithwaite Wife Hole** seen on the walk between the **Hill Inn** and **Ingleborough**.

Although limestone is the most obvious rock, we frequently come across *gritstone,* which is a hard form of sandstone. This is another *sedimentary* rock, formed by the mud settling out of river deltas, and in the Three Peaks area the *gritstone* was laid down on top of the limestone. Erosion, mainly by glaciers, stripped off most of this overlayer of stone, leaving successive bands of limestone and *gritstone*. This can be seen quite clearly by looking at **Ingleborough** or **Pen y Ghent**, where bands of different rock types have formed vertical escarpments.

All this may seem to be of academic interest, especially for those who just want to get out to walk the Yorkshire Three Peaks Challenge, but the geology is with us wherever we go and not just in the differences in the scenery. The well-drained limestone landscape often gives us drier walking than the less well-drained peat moors of *gritstone* country, as we will find on different parts of the walks in this guide.

The other striking difference found in the different rock types is the grip they provide - highly relevant in our case, because we are walking amongst and over both limestone and *gritstone*. Limestone provides ample friction when dry, but it's a completely different matter when wet. *Limestone pavements* in wet conditions are places to exercise great care, as they are both slippery and criss-crossed by ankle breaking *grikes*. *Gritstone*, on the other hand, gives superb friction, even when wet. In the places where stone causeways have been laid to repair paths, gritstone has been used, sometimes flown in by helicopter, rather than the hardwearing but slippery limestone.

NATURAL HISTORY

Early-purple orchid, near Southerscales

The limestone of the Dales also influences the plants that grow there. Wherever you go there are plants of interest to the botanist, but the finest area of all is on the route between the **Hill Inn** and **Ingleborough**. Here we pass through two nature reserves; the **Southerscales Nature Reserve** and the **Ingleborough National Nature Reserve**.

From the **Hill Inn**, we start on the thinner drier soils of the limestone grasslands. The most common wildflower species here is purple wild thyme, while in spring early-purple orchids are frequently seen. In summer the yellow rock rose is in flower, followed by delicate blue harebells.

As we proceed on our route, the lower grasslands are succeeded by the *limestone pavement*, which holds a variety of wildflowers. Although **Southerscales** has a managed grazing regime to allow wildflowers to grow, the *clints* and *grikes* have their own inbuilt grazing management - the fissures of the *grikes* provide cool, sheltered conditions, out of reach of grazing animals, and wood anemones and bluebells may be seen. Several varieties of fern also thrive in these conditions.

The wetter conditions of the moorland above **Braithwaite Wife Hole** favour the more acid-loving plants including heath rush, purple moor grass and sphagnum moss. Ornithologists aren't left out either, and should be on the lookout for the wheatear and skylark. Those with a deeper interest in the plants and wildlife of the area should look at the website for the Yorkshire Dales National Park Authority (www.yorkshiredales.org.uk).

HUMAN INFLUENCE

If nature shaped the Yorkshire Dales initially, man has continued the work since. Long before humans arrived on the scene, the area was the home to animals that are now found in warmer regions. Bones dated at 130,000 years old and found in Victoria Cave at nearby **Settle** include those of hippos, narrow-nosed rhinos, elephants and spotted hyenas. After the last Ice Age, the cave was occupied by hibernating brown bears, and an antler harpoon point was discovered in amongst reindeer bones. At 11,000 years old, this is the earliest evidence of human activity in the Yorkshire Dales, probably by nomadic hunters.

The first settlers probably arrived about 7,000 years ago. At another nearby site at **Giggleswick**, human bones over 5,000 years old were found in a cave, together with the bones of domestic cattle, sheep and pigs. Experts believe that the bones may have been used in some kind of ritual, suggesting that humans were well established in the area by then. The stone tools used in this period were subsequently replaced by metal tools, with the introduction of bronze at about 2,500 BC followed by iron at about 600 BC.

The best known of these iron-using people were the Celtic Brigantes, the first humans in the area of whom there is a written record. Although mainly living in small farming settlements, they were also capable of large-scale organisation. The most obvious example of this is a place we'll visit more than once - the summit of **Ingleborough**.

On the summit plateau the Brigantes built a hill fort with a stone rampart 1,000 metres long. Traces of more than twenty circular huts can still be found, though the rampart has been damaged over the years, latterly by walkers taking stones to make cairns. The Brigantes dominated this area until the Romans defeated them in 74 AD. By this time, little of the area we now know as the Yorkshire Dales was in a truly natural state, many woods having been cleared for agriculture.

The Roman occupation lasted for over 300 hundred years. They did settle in parts of the area, but their main legacy lies in the straight roads they left, one example being the Roman road leading from **Ribblehead** to the Roman fort at **Bainbridge** in Wensleydale. In other parts of the Yorkshire Dales the Romans left traces of their marching camps, but there's virtually no evidence of their occupation in the local place names. The British tribes who co-existed with the Romans did, however, leave some of their place names, the most obvious example being the name of one of the Three Peaks, **Pen y Ghent** ("Hill of the Winds"). But the next wave of invaders was not long in coming.

The Anglo-Saxons defeated the British tribes around 600 AD, and the Yorkshire Dales area was incorporated into the English kingdom of Northumbria. Place names do survive from this period; settlements with names ending in –*ham* or –*ton* have Anglo-Saxon links, such as **Ingleton** at the foot of **Ingleborough**, or **Horton in Ribblesdale** near **Pen y Ghent**. However, the Anglo-Saxons had barely had time to get their feet under the table when the next wave of invaders arrived.

In 865 AD a massive Danish army invaded the north of England, conquering Northumbria in little more than a decade. By 900 AD the Danes were followed by Viking invaders from Ireland, and both groups settled extensively in the area. There are reminders by the dozen of the Scandinavian occupation of Yorkshire.

Any settlement name ending in –*by* has a Danish origin, such as **Ireby** near **Ingleton**. It was the Vikings, though, who left place names and words still in use in modern Yorkshire, including *fell* (hill), *thwaite* (clearing), *scales* (summer pasture), *beck* (stream), *gill* (ravine or gorge), *force* (waterfall), *tarn* (small lake), scar (crag), and *dale* (valley).

The last invaders to come this way were the Normans, following their conquest of Britain in 1066. They found Yorkshire to be a rebellious part of their new kingdom. William the Conqueror embarked on a campaign which the Normans called, "Harrying of the North". A scorched earth policy resulted in 100,000 English dying of famine, but the rebels were brought to heel, and Yorkshire became as much a part of Norman England as any other county.

The feudal system was introduced by the Normans, where the Lord ruled the land and the peasants farmed it, and traces of the medieval field systems can still be seen in parts of the Dales.

Ancient drystone wall below Whernside

Feudalism gradually gave way to a system of tenancy, where it was in the interests of the tenant farmer to build a more substantial house. From the 17th Century onwards the wooden houses of the poorer classes were gradually replaced by the stone farmhouses that dot the landscape today.

The next major impact on the scenery of the Dales came in mid-eighteenth century, with the Enclosure Acts. The drystone walls, built without mortar and typical of the area, were built at this time to enclose what was previously common land. After the enclosures, sheep farming became a major industry.

Sheep farming - an important industry in the Yorkshire Dales for centuries

The Carlisle to Settle railway, Ingleborough rising behind

The final large-scale changes to the Dales scenery came with the Industrial Revolution. The limestone that is a dominant feature of the landscape was also seen as having commercial value, and large scale quarrying was started, some of which continues to this day.

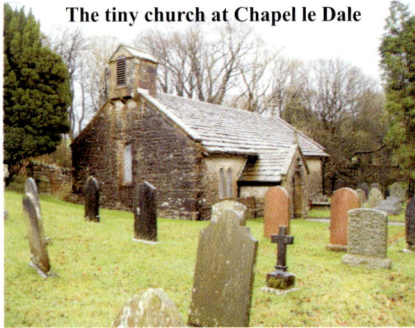

The tiny church at Chapel le Dale

The Industrial Revolution also brought the railway in the form of the **Settle** to **Carlisle** rail line. The building of the line was typical of the drive and determination of the Victorians, although it came at a heavy cost in human life.

Many of the navvies who died as a result of accident or sickness are buried at the tiny church at **Chapel le Dale**, where there is also a memorial plaque.

The Ribblehead Viaduct

The most impressive monument, however, is the **Ribblehead Viaduct** itself. The viaduct is 400 meters long with 24 arches, and was completed in 1874 after five years of building. It is a feature of the landscape that we'll get to know much better as we walk the routes that culminate in the Yorkshire Three Peaks Challenge.

FIRST THINGS FIRST

Hill walking in Britain is unique. We don't have the higher altitude of some mountain regions in other parts of the world, but we do have latitude - The Scottish Highlands are at the same latitude as Moscow, and North Yorkshire is not a lot further south than that. Our proximity to the Atlantic means we generally get warmer weather in winter than Moscow, but with a tendency towards rapidly changing weather systems, the main features being wet, windy and cool conditions.

It isn't always as warm as this ..

It's possible on the right day to walk the Yorkshire Three Peaks Challenge in perfect weather, wearing just shorts and a T-shirt. On the other hand, you may meet the same conditions that a group of friends and I did when I was a teenager. A photograph of us

Suitable clothing for most hill days

on the summit of **Ingleborough** taken in early spring, shows an ominous grey cloud in the near background. Within twenty minutes we were in an unexpectedly violent snowstorm. We wandered all around the perimeter of the summit plateau, failing to locate three different ways off. In the end we retreated to the summit shelter, and sat out the storm. Half an hour later we finally found a way down. On the way we met several people going up wearing - yes, shorts and T-shirts!

Having said that, the Yorkshire Three Peaks Challenge is an ideal first route for those who wish to try a challenge walk or long distance route. Although the walk feels remote, you are never very far from the road, which you cross at **Ribblehead** and **Chapel-le-Dale**. Both places have public houses, where you can get hot food and drinks, or even order a taxi home if you wish to abandon the walk.

Those attempting the Yorkshire Three Peaks Challenge come in all shapes, sizes and age groups. The other big variable is experience, so the following section contains advice on what clothing and equipment you may need on the walk, how to find your way around, and what to do if things go wrong. Although the advice is primarily for those with little or no experience of British hill walking, there are snippets of information that may be of use to all.

CLOTHING & EQUIPMENT

Although lower than some of the other uplands areas of Britain, the Yorkshire

Dales can throw a wide variety of weather your way, so clothing and kit for hill use has to be able to cope with wide range of conditions. The conventional system for clothing uses a layer system to trap air; air is an insulator, and that's what keeps you warm. These layers comprise a *base layer*, *insulation layer* and *shell layer*.

The *base layer* is a thin layer worn next to the skin, which can transmit moisture away from skin to the outer layers. Wool and silk *base layers* are still the most efficient, as they stay warm when wet, but there can be problems with comfort, price and the care needed to look after them. Man-made alternatives are better (Helly Hensen "Lifa" clothing is typical) as they work almost as well, last longer and are easier to look after. Cotton is very poor, as it does not transmit moisture away, and destroys insulation by replacing air with moisture.

Walker wearing insulating layer

The *insulation layer* worn above the *base* layer is the one that actually keeps us warm. Again, wool is very good but suffers the same disadvantages as above. Modern man-made fleeces are best, as they are warm, lightweight, transmit moisture to the outer layer helping to keep the body dry, and they dry quickly if wet.

The shell layer keeps the insulating layer dry

The *shell layer* is a waterproof and /or windproof layer worn over the insulation layer. Not all fleeces are windproof, so they need to be protected by the shell layer to prevent warmth being lost. Breathable waterproofs (e.g. Goretex, Event, etc) are the best option, and they will also keep out the wind. The idea is to continue transmitting moisture away from the insulation layer, and breathable garments can do this to some extent.

The above advice applies mainly to the torso. When choosing trousers the same principles apply, but not quite as much insulation is needed, especially in milder conditions. Jeans are definitely out. They absorb water, take ages to dry, and soak away body heat in the drying process. They are, in effect, working in the same way that a fridge does, using body heat to evaporate the moisture, leading to a high risk of *hypothermia*. Modern walking / trekking trousers or leggings are the best choice.

As well as covering our bodies we mustn't forget the head and hands. A hat conserves a great deal of heat - over 50% of our body heat can be lost through the uncovered head. A hat can also be used to help regulate body temperature by allowing more or less heat to escape, instead of removing a layer of clothing. There's an old walkers' saying; "If you want to keep your feet warm, put a hat on". This is because the body abandons extremities such as feet when it is cold in order to preserve the core temperature. Also don't forget gloves. Keep them dry, carry spares in very cold conditions, and NEVER put them down onto snow, as this soaks away the heat in the glove - tuck them inside your jacket instead.

Finally, we mustn't forget the feet. Supportive boots are preferred, as they protect the feet and ankles in rough terrain. A good sole pattern that provides grip is also important. New boots should always be worn in before setting off on longer walks.

Comfortable, worn-in boots

To summarise, ideal wear for all but the coldest conditions would comprise :-

- base layer vest
- micro-fleece shirt
- fleece jacket or pullover
- walking / trekking trousers (suitable for the conditions you'll encounter - ask when buying) or leggings
- breathable waterproof shell (jacket and trousers)
- hat & gloves (in pocket or rucksack)
- supportive boots (but not too heavy)

.. a rucksack or backpack of the correct size ..

In hot conditions consideration should be given to protection from the sun, including hats and sunscreen.

Any of these layers can be removed or replaced to cope with varying conditions. This means that clothing needs to be carried somehow when not being worn. In addition there are also other things to carry. The best solution is a rucksack or backpack of the correct size (20-30 litres).

For a simple day walk, the rucksack should contain the following :-

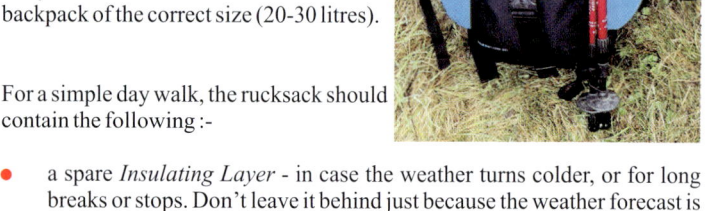

- a spare *Insulating Layer* - in case the weather turns colder, or for long breaks or stops. Don't leave it behind just because the weather forecast is good.

- a map and compass - it may seem to be over doing things to take these along when you have the Walk! Guide or even a GPS with you, but they give a good picture of the area if the route has to be changed. Even GPS users need a map for reference, or as backup if the GPS stops working. It goes without saying that it's important to know how to use them.

- a GPS is a sensible item to carry, as it removes much of the uncertainty of navigation, but as with the map, ensure you know how to use it. A copy of **GPS The Easy Way** by Discovery Walking Guides is a good investment for those new to GPS. Spare batteries for the GPS are also a good idea.

- a basic first aid kit plus some knowledge of how to use it.

- a whistle to send a distress signal in case of emergency (see Emergency Procedure below)

- a torch, preferably a head-torch - essential for walking if it gets dark, and it can also be used for a distress signal.

- a "bivibag" - at its simplest, this is a heavy gauge plastic bag, big enough for one person to get into in an emergency, keeping out the wet and wind. They are lightweight and cheap.

- a mobile phone - if there are several in the group, switch off all but one. Don't waste power on frivolous calls, and equally don't rely on always having a signal, especially in the valleys.

- food and drink - high calorie, sugary food will keep you going longer, together with water or a commercial hydration liquid; at least a litre should be carried in most conditions, and hot drinks carried in cold conditions. Drink frequently - if you start to feel thirsty you are already dehydrated, and dehydration will make you feel tired. There's a simple test for dehydration (those of a sensitive nature should turn away at this point). This is to check the colour of your urine when you pee - light or straw coloured is fine, darker yellow means you are starting to become dehydrated, orange or brown means very dehydrated - get some liquid down at once.

- and finally, don't forget a watch; essential for pub opening and closing times, but also a very important navigational instrument.

NAVIGATION

Navigation on the Yorkshire Three Peaks Challenge is usually fairly simple. The route follows well-defined paths for the most part, and on a summer weekend you may have lots of company in the form of others also attempting the Challenge. This doesn't automatically guarantee trouble free navigation,

These will keep us on course

however. You may be presented with a multiple choice of paths, and the group you are following may turn out to be walking the Pennine Way, which is just a bit longer than our intended walk!

This guide should keep you on the straight and narrow. Used in conjunction with a GPS you shouldn't have any problems, but carrying a map and compass is a good insurance policy, and doesn't weigh much or take up too much space. It is beyond the scope of this book to present a course on mountain navigation, but a few pointers may be helpful.

We will mainly be following clear paths; in the world of map reading these are known as navigation *handrails*. Along the *handrail* there will be obvious features, such as path junctions, bridges over streams, etc. These can be identified as we pass them, and are known as *tick off features*; keeping tabs on what we have passed gives a good idea of whereabouts we are on the route.

It's also useful to identify a feature that will tell us if we have gone too far, such as a road or stream crossing our path. This is known as a *collecting feature*. When using the map or guidebook it can be helpful to fold the map, or open the book, so that a small area is in use, then to keep the thumb on the *tick off feature* we have just passed. This is known as *thumbing*. By using some or all of the above simple techniques, we should be able to keep tabs on our position on the route.

Lost?

Checking the map

Everyone gets lost (or "slightly misplaced!") sooner or later, and the ones who say that they don't are probably being economical with the truth! So, if you do get "slightly misplaced" don't panic - stop, have a cup of coffee, and, talk things through as a group. If all else fails, turn round and go back to a known safe point.

If that's not possible, follow obvious, well-used paths heading the way you need to go, but make sure that the direction you choose isn't heading towards large uninhabited areas (open moorland, etc). Head for roads or habitations if possible.

If you are high and see what appears to be safe ground or good path below, don't go rushing straight down to it if you can't see all of the ground between you and safety. This is known as "The Lure of the Descent", and can be hazardous, because you have stopped making decisions. Try not to get lost in first place - spend time usefully by navigating accurately, using the guidebook, GPS, map or all three.

IF THINGS START TO GO WRONG

The walks in this book do not pass through dangerous or hazardous terrain, and thousands of people walk here every year without incident. It is always possible, though, that despite your best preparations, things may start to unravel a bit. Here are some bits of advice to help you in the unlikely event you have problems.

Tired

Avoid tiredness by adequate training beforehand; in particular, learn to pace yourself. Make sure you eat adequately before setting off on the walk. If you become tired on the walk, tell your mates how you feel, stop and have some high calorie food and a drink. If you are absolutely exhausted, keep warm, get into shelter, get some calories in, then carry on when you are feeling better. Make sure you have occasional rest stops, but don't dawdle!

Adverse Weather

Check the weather forecast before setting off. Watch for signs of adverse changes in the predicted weather, and make early decisions to change the route if necessary. If there is a severe deterioration in the weather, consider abandoning the walk. Get to a lower altitude, using safe paths or ground, but remember not to fall for the "Lure of the descent". If you are unable to move get into shelter, using your emergency bivibag if nothing else is available.

Injuries & Illness

Injuries and illnesses are most unlikely, though they can range from blisters or sprains at one extreme to fractures at the other. Prevention is always better than cure, so take care where appropriate. For example, slow down when crossing bits of slippery wet *limestone pavement*, or better still avoid them; a short detour is better than a fractured ankle.

In the case of minor injuries or illness, carry out appropriate First Aid, and then carry on with the walk if possible, otherwise head for safety. If injuries or illnesses are more serious get the whole group into shelter, carry out First Aid and get help (see below).

ANY fracture is a serious injury, so in the case of a suspected fracture, on no account should the injured person attempt to walk off - aggravating a fracture by excessive movement is a sure way to make a bad job worse.

A good insurance policy

A combination of cold, wet conditions plus exhaustion and anxiety can lead to *hypothermia* or *exposure*. This is easily prevented by wearing the right clothing, eating well, and building up fitness. The symptoms are easy to remember - the person affected "mumbles, grumbles, stumbles and tumbles."

Extroverts become quiet, shy characters become vocal or even aggressive, and those affected often display bizarre behaviour, such as discarding clothing or equipment.

Hypothermia is a medical emergency. If the above symptoms are presented, and help is nearby and the casualty is still mobile, the walk should be abandoned and the group should head to a safe location. If this isn't an option, the casualty should be placed in a bivibag, insulated from the ground, and dressed with extra warm clothing if available. Assistance should be sought IMMEDIATELY.

Getting Help on the Hills

It is always worth trying to sort things out without help if possible, as this is less of a drain on expensive resources, and it is more satisfying for us to be able to sort out our own problems. However, where there is no alternative, do not hesitate to seek help. Local mountain rescue teams are volunteers, with jobs, families and hobbies to get on with, but the reason they volunteer in the first place is an indication of their dedication and willingness to help.

If Help is Required ..

Use a mobile phone if there is a signal. If you don't have a signal try anyway, as all service providers accept incoming emergency calls. Phone 999 or 112 and ask for "North Yorkshire Police" (you may be connected initially to a call centre in another county, who would connect you to their local police). When you are connected to the police, ask for Mountain Rescue. The police will need to know the following :- what has happened, the incident location, when did the incident happen, the number of people involved, and the weather in the area.

If you can't phone, consider sending for help - at least two people should go for help together, with at least one to stay with the casualty. The remainder of the group should either go down to safety, or help with the casualty as appropriate. It's worth bearing in mind that people sat about the hillside in bad weather may become cold whilst waiting for help. Those going for help should have the same information to pass on as above. Of course, this assumes that you are walking in a group. Those walking alone need to be extra careful and self-reliant.

If you think that someone might be nearby, use the recognised distress signal. This is six long whistle blasts, wait one minute, then repeat. With a torch use six long flashes, wait one minute, then repeat. The reply to a distress signal is three whistle blasts (or three torch flashes) - if you hear a reply, keep signalling. NEVER use a whistle unless in an emergency - a rescue team may be called out unintentionally.

To summarise - wear the correct clothing, carry the correct gear, and you can't go far wrong. If things do go wrong, don't panic, remember the advice above, and use the gear that you are carrying.

PREPARATION

So, we now know a bit more about the Three Peaks area, the kind of gear we will need and how to go about the walks safely. All we need to do now is get fitter, plan how we will tackle the Challenge and sort out the organisation. Some of the ideas below will give you the possibility of a much bigger and more enjoyable project than just completing the Challenge walk. However, for those who can't spare the time, or just want to get straight on with the Challenge, there are all sorts of helpful hints to enhance the chance of success on the day.

GETTING FIT

Unfortunately, being fit enough for the Challenge isn't one of the optional extras. Those who are not physically active need to make a start at least three months before the date of the Challenge walk, longer if possible. If fortunate enough to live near a gym, you could have a personalised training plan drawn up, but here are a few ideas for a DIY regime. NOTE - if you are completely unfit, it would be wise to have a medical check up before starting any training.

Striding down green lanes ..

The first place to start is with basic fitness. Try three sessions a week, with a day off in between. About 45 minutes of brisk walking is good for starters, with 5 minutes at either end to warm up and cool down.

If this becomes easy, introduce jogging or running. After a couple of weeks include undulating or hilly ground into the training schedule.

After a month of that, it's time to build up stamina - this is

.. whatever the walk, it's all training.

.. alongside canals ..

done by progressively increasing the effort required in our training, so carry more weight than you would usually, and find a walk that involves hilly ground if possible. When that gets easier, increase the distance and the weight carried. There are few parts of the country that are completely flat, so for most this shouldn't be a problem.

After a month of working on stamina, the next stage is to build up some hill fitness. For one of the weekly training days, try to get to a walking area with more hills, such as the outskirts of the Peak District or the Downs. Again, such areas are within reasonable travelling distance for most of us, from Cornwall to Northumbria.

There's lots of training opportunities, from Cornwall ..

.. through Mid-Wales ..

To summarise; as a minimum try to spend a month on basic fitness work for three days a week, then a month of stamina training carrying some weight, then a final month replacing one of the weekly training days with an easy hill walk.

.. and Derbyshire ..

After working up for three months, it's worthwhile travelling to Yorkshire to try one of the first three walks in this guide.

.. to Northumbria.

Compare your time with the time allowed in the book, and if you are able to at least equal the book time, it's probably time to start on the rest of the walks in this guide.

PLANNING - THE STRATEGY

The concept of this guide is to maximise the chance of succeeding on the

Challenge walk by prior preparation. Getting fit is part of that preparation, but by completing the first six walks in this book before taking on the Challenge itself, we will have a good prior knowledge of the route, and will probably also have experienced a wide range of conditions beforehand.

Many of those who wish to take part in the Three Peaks Challenge do not live within convenient travel distance of the area. So, why not set up a weekly base camp in Yorkshire. A good location for this would be **Horton in Ribblesdale**. **Horton** is blessed with two pubs, two campsites, a bunk barn, and B & B accommodation. It's also handy as a base for all the preparatory walks, in fact all the walks in this book have been devised to be convenient for a Horton base. There are also pubs, bunk barns and B&Bs within easy reach at **Ribblehead** and **Chapel le Dale**.

A base camp?

A suggested timetable for those living some distance away would be to travel to **Horton** on a Friday evening, do one of the walks on the Saturday, enjoy one of the great pubs in the area on Saturday night, and either get a second walk in on Sunday before travelling home, or perhaps do a shorter walk or some sightseeing. The majority of the population of Britain live within about five hours or so of **Horton** (London 5 hours, Bristol 4, Norwich 5½, Newcastle 3, Edinburgh 4½).

Although this might appear to be a little drawn out, it gives a great opportunity to get to know the area intimately. Start the Yorkshire phase in late spring, and by the end of summer you will not only have completed the Yorkshire Three Peaks Challenge, you will also have gained an in-depth knowledge of the area in a very short time and you will be regulars at your favourite pub and accommodation.

THE DAY OF THE CHALLENGE - TACTICS

However you decide to prepare beforehand, tactics on the day can make a big difference, both in the enjoyment of the walk, and even in its success. The Challenge route traditionally starts and ends at the **Pen y Ghent Café**, with the advantage of using their booking in and out system. Complete the walk within twelve hours and you become eligible for membership of the Three Peaks Club. If none of those factors matter, then the Challenge route could also be started at **Ribblehead** or the **Hill Inn**.

When to go?

The next thing to consider is when to tackle the Challenge. Mid summer is probably best, as this gives ample time to work up to the big day, and also leaves time available for further attempts in the event of failure. The most important advantage, though, is in the hours of daylight. Between 21 March and 21 September we have twelve-hour days, and by mid June the hours of daylight are even longer. We also want the best weather possible for the big day.

Size of Group?

Another consideration is the size of group, with the ideal being 4 to 6. Fewer than 4 has safety implications – if someone is injured an individual might have to go for help alone (remember the safety section in "First things first"). More than 6 can become very unwieldy. The larger the group, the more variation there will be in fitness, walking speeds, etc. Having said all that, it is not unusual to find couples or even individuals completing the Challenge. It does mean, though, that extra care should be taken - a sprained ankle is more than a mere inconvenience to a solo walker.

Supported, semi-supported or not?

The final tactical consideration is whether to do the walk supported or unsupported. A supported attempt would use a vehicle with a dedicated driver. This vehicle carries extra water, food and any spare kit between sections, giving the possibility of the walkers shedding some weight. The vehicle is also useful in the event of tiredness or injury, giving a means of leaving the walk. The support vehicle goes to **Ribblehead** first of all, and when the party starts the next section the vehicle goes to the **Hill Inn**.

The Challenge can also be done "semi-supported", by parking one vehicle with water and spare gear at the lay-by near the **Hill Inn**. This vehicle could also act as an ambulance if needed, being in easy walking distance of **Ribblehead** and at the end of the second section of the Challenge route. Completely unsupported is also an option, and could be considered the purest. If this alternative is followed, it is still possible to reduce the weight carried by caching water at **Ribblehead** and the **Hill Inn**; at least 1 litre per person should be left. It's probably best to hide it, to be sure that it will be there on our arrival, and empty containers should be collected after the event.

TIPS FOR SUCCESS

There are lots of ways in which we can ensure an enjoyable and successful Challenge day. Here are a few :-

- Use the practice walks to get used to your gear – This will help us to learn how to reduce weight on the big day by only carrying what is essential.

- Keep hydrated on the walk, but don't waste energy by carrying water - cache it instead.

- Take light, energy providing snacks, keep them handy, and eat on the move - try these on the practice walks, to make sure you get on with them.

- Pick the optimum weather conditions - if the weather is absolutely foul, consider a day in the pub or sightseeing, and return on another weekend.

- Don't rush on the big day, especially at the beginning - if you find that you are getting in advance of the guidebook times, slow down. You can always speed up towards the end if energy allows.

- On the other hand, don't dawdle. Don't linger at the road crossing points, as this is where you will lose time. Steady progress will win the day, rather than rushing then needing frequent rest stops.

- Use this guide, but adapt it according to your experiences on the practice walks. Where there are possible time saving options we have researched them for you - to pinch the Co-op's slogan; "We go further so you don't have to".

- Finally, make use of the **Pen y Ghent Café** clock out and in facility (See "Accommodation"). If you have problems, at least someone knows where you are.

Finally, don't forget the Countryside Code :-

Be safe - plan ahead and follow any signs
Even when going out locally, it's best to get the latest information about where and when you can go; for example, your rights to go onto some areas of open land may be restricted while work is carried out, for safety reasons or during breeding seasons. Follow advice and local signs, and be prepared for the unexpected.

Leave gates and property as you find them
Please respect the working life of the countryside, as our actions can affect people's livelihoods, our heritage, and the safety and welfare of animals and ourselves.

Protect plants and animals, and take your litter home
We have a responsibility to protect our countryside now and for future generations, so make sure you don't harm animals, birds, plants, or trees.

Keep dogs under close control
The countryside is a great place to exercise dogs, but it's every owner's duty to make sure their dog is not a danger or nuisance to farm animals, wildlife or other people.

Consider other people
Showing consideration and respect for other people makes the countryside a pleasant environment for everyone - at home, at work and at leisure.

WALK LOCATION MAPS

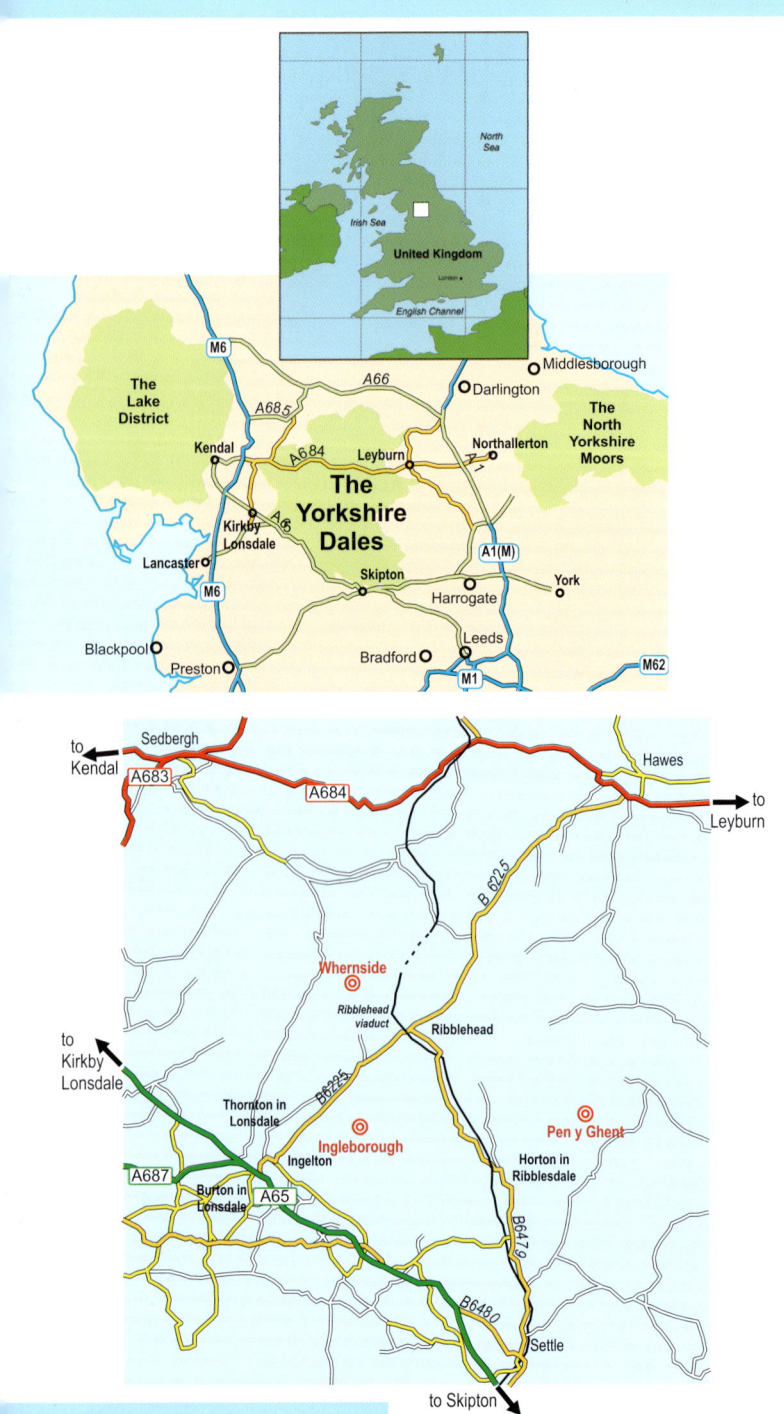

32 Yorkshire 3 Peaks

SYMBOLS RATING GUIDE

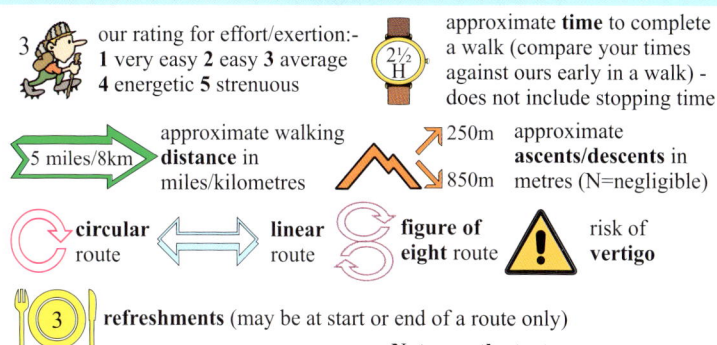

3 our rating for effort/exertion:-
1 very easy **2** easy **3** average
4 energetic **5** strenuous

approximate **time** to complete a walk (compare your times against ours early in a walk) - does not include stopping time

5 miles/8km — approximate walking **distance** in miles/kilometres

250m / 850m — approximate **ascents/descents** in metres (N=negligible)

circular route

linear route

figure of eight route

risk of **vertigo**

refreshments (may be at start or end of a route only)

- Walk descriptions include:
- timing in minutes, shown as (40M)
- compass directions, shown as (NW)
- heights in metres, shown as (1355m)
- GPS waypoints, shown as (Wp.3)

Notes on the text
Place names are shown in **bold text**, except where we refer to a written sign, when they are enclosed in single quotation marks. Local or unusual words are shown in *italics*, and are explained in the accompanying text.

ORDNANCE SURVEY MAPPING

All the map sections in **The Yorkshire Three Peaks Challenge** are from the latest Ordnance Survey digital mapping at 25,000 scale (Explorer series) and licenced for publication under Licence Number 40044851.

Each map section is aligned so that north is at the top of the page on which the map section appears. Y3P walking routes are shown as a dashed red line drawn alongside the OS map features. Each waypoint referred to in the detailed walk descriptions is shown as a waypoint number with a red arrow showing the exact location of the waypoint on the map section.

All the map sections are subject to the Ordnance Survey copyright.

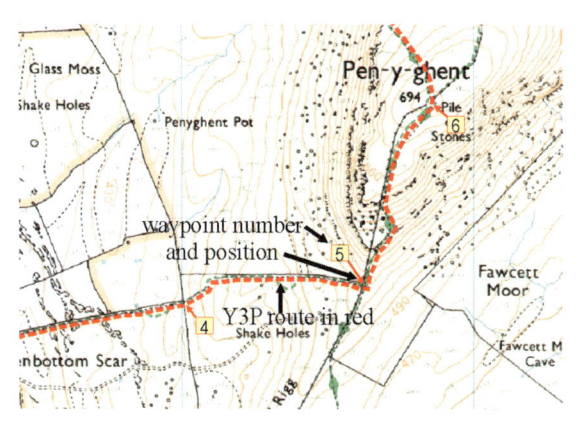

USING GPS AS A NAVIGATIONAL AID
by David Brawn (author, GPS The Easy Way)

A successful Challenge on 'The Yorkshire Three Peaks' requires you to complete the three summits and return to your start point (usually, but not always, the Pen y Ghent café)within twelve hours. Success is dependent on two main factors:

- **Fitness**; being fit enough to complete the three summits quick enough for potential success.
- **Navigation**; getting from your start point up to the top of the summits and down again without getting lost or delayed.

Paul has produced six 'day walks' that you can use as fitness training, as well as his full 'Challenge' route, but however fit you are it is of little use if you are going in the wrong direction.

IMPORTANCE OF ACCURATE NAVIGATION

Accurate navigation is vital if you are to succeed on the challenge. Its also important on any hiking adventure if you are to avoid the dispiriting experience of taking a wrong turn, then finding you have gone wrong and having to backtrack onto your correct route.

Whatever you might think of traditional 'Map & Compass' navigation, GPS is the most accurate navigation system for outdoor adventuring.

GPS NAVIGATION

GPS units give an accuracy of approx 5 metres on **The Yorkshire Three Peaks** walking routes when you have good satellite reception; which will be almost all of the time depending upon the configuration of satellites at the time you are walking. Paul's waypoints, which are included in 'GPS Waypoints & Coordinates' on pages 86 & 87, can be loaded into your GPS unit memory and called up for each walking route; or you could load all the waypoints as one file in your GPS unit memory. Just using the waypoints will tell you when you are reaching the points described in Paul's walk descriptions and shown on the OS map sections, very reassuring to know exactly where you are and that you are on the correct route.

Paul's GPS records are available from DWG on our **Personal Navigator Files CD version 6.01** onwards in file formats compatible with Memory-Map and a wide range of GPS software along with Google Earth files, enabling you to see **The Yorkshire Three Peaks** walking routes in real time.

GPS will provide you with the 'pinpoint' navigational accuracy that could be all important to the success of your Challenge, but it's advisable to:-

- familiarise yourself with GPS through a book such as **GPS The Easy Way** or **GPS for Walkers** and,
- use your GPS (and software) regularly so that you become familiar with its use and accuracy.

- Once you get into regular use you'll find your GPS does much more than just tell you where you are as it records where you have been and with pre-loaded Tracks and Waypoints can show you where you want to go.

GPS & SAT-NAV EQUIPMENT

- Equipment doesn't have to be expensive to give you 'pinpoint' navigational accuracy. GPS units range from Garmin eTrexH basic at £70, now with improved chipset giving faster processing of satellite signals, through more advanced models with extra functions. My choice is for a GPS with PC connectivity enabling me to use a variety of GPS software such as GPS Utility, Oziexplorer and Memory-Map and even with this spec, you are unlikely to spend above £150. MemoryMap Adventurer 2800 is a full mapping GPSs giving you a moving OS map display and costs around £260. These are 'pocket money' prices compared to the time and expense you will put into your Challenge and a bargain if they assist in your success.

- The key to GPS and Sat-Nav is to understand your equipment, use it regularly so you are familiar with its use.

INPUTTING GPS WAYPOINTS FOR THE YORKSHIRE THREE PEAKS

- GPS Waypoints are quoted for the OSGB datum and BNG position format. To input the Waypoints into your GPS we suggest that you:-

- switch on your GPS and select 'simulator', 'demo' or 'operate with GPS off' mode,

- check that your GPS is set to the OSGB datum and the BNG position format; see your GPS manual for instructions,

- input the GPS Waypoints into a 'GPS route' with the same number as the walking route number; then there should be no confusion as to which walking route it refers,

- repeat the inputting of routes until you have covered all your planned walking routes,

- turn off your GPS. When you turn the GPS back on it should return to its normal navigation mode.

Note that GPS Waypoints complement the detailed walking route descriptions, and are not intended for use as an alternative to the route description.

MAKING A START - THREE PEAKS, ONE AT A TIME

Pen y Ghent in the early morning

If you are new to walking in the Yorkshire Dales, you're in for a treat, as we trace our way up each of the three Peaks. First though, we will do them one at a time, giving a chance to savour the experience, as well as getting to know the area.

For those who are already familiar with the Yorkshire Three Peaks these are routes well worth repeating, time and time again; three great hills with three classic routes up them.

1 PEN Y GHENT FROM HORTON IN RIBBLESDALE

Horton Lane, Pen y Ghent ahead

Pen y Ghent is the lowest of the Three Peaks, at 694 metres, but size isn't everything, and in the opinion of many it is the most interesting of the Big Three. The route starts from **Horton in Ribblesdale**, and joins the Pennine Way to reach the summit from the south.

There is one short section where we may have to use our hands, but there is no great difficulty and the top is reached with a real sense of achievement. From there it's an easy descent back to **Horton**, with great views of **Whernside** and **Ingleborough** on the way. The name **Pen y Ghent** is an echo of times long past, and is a survival of the ancient Cumbric language, similar to Old Welsh, which died out around the twelfth century. It means "Hill of the Winds".

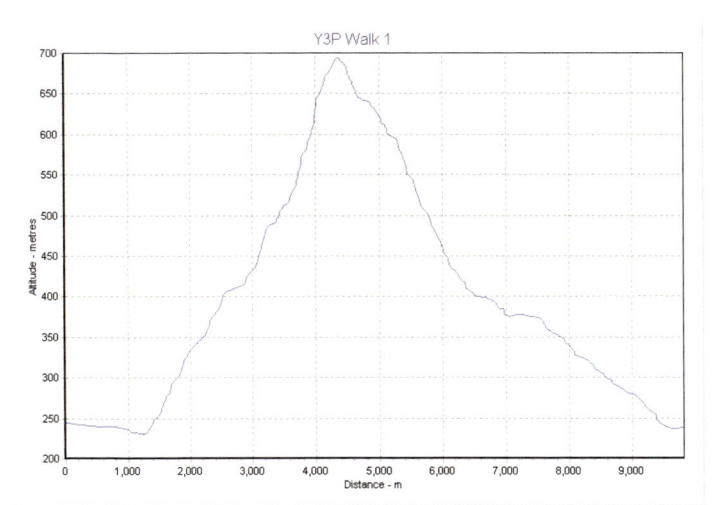

4 | 3¼ H | 5.8 miles 9.31km | 488m / 488m | ↻ | 4

Y3P Walk 1

Access by car: The walk starts at **Horton in Ribblesdale**. For most, the easiest approach by car is to head for **Settle** on the A65, and from there to take the B6479 from **Settle** to **Ribblehead**. The alternative road route is to take the B6255 **Hawes** to **Ingleton** road, turning off at **Ribblehead** to **Horton**. The main car park is clearly signed, and has a toilet building. Parking for a day is quite reasonably priced – regard it as putting something back into the local economy. **Horton in Ribblesdale** is also on the **Settle** to **Carlisle** railway line, making a car-free trip possible.

We join the main road by the car park (Wp.1 0M) and walk in the direction of Settle (S) passing the **Pen y Ghent Café**. The road bends to the left at the **Golden Lion**, with the church of **St Oswald** on the left. Just beyond the church there are two minor roads on the left. We ignore the first, signed as a dead end, and cross the road bridge over the beck to the second road (Wp.2 8M).

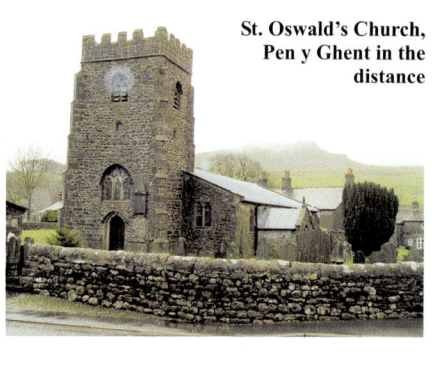

St. Oswald's Church, Pen y Ghent in the distance

Our route follows this lane with the beck on the left, passing the village school on the right. A little further on, the lane moves to the right away from the beck, heading towards **Brackenbottom** farmhouse. As we arrive at **Brackenbottom** (Wp.3 20M) the route follows a footpath on the left, immediately before the first building, and signed to 'Pen y Ghent'. After passing through a wooden gate, the path heads upwards (NE) with a stone wall running parallel on our left.

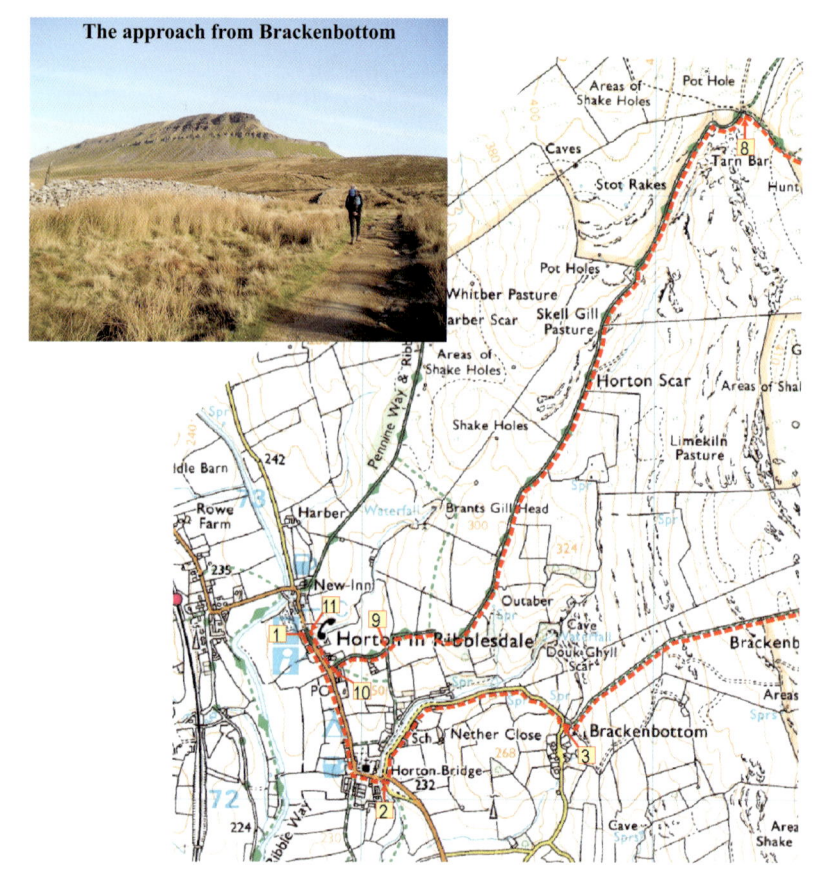

The approach from Brackenbottom

Our path then crosses a wall by a step stile, and continues gaining height (ENE) with the wall still on our left, passing through a small limestone outcrop and over another step stile. Our route continues through two more small limestone outcrops, following a constructed path to a wooden gate in the wall (Wp.4 53M).

The path continues briefly without an adjacent wall, then after a little over 100 metres rejoins a wall running parallel on the left side of our path, still gaining height. In places the path has been rebuilt using flat causeway stones. These have been used in several places on the Yorkshire Three Peak Challenge route to combat the serious erosion that had become a problem over the years. Although unpopular with some and regarded as an intrusion, they are a pragmatic solution and the stones blend in well with their surroundings. After a short steeper section, another wall crosses our path, and we come to a wooden gate (Wp.5 72M) where we join the **Pennine Way**.

Here we turn left and continue upwards on a well-constructed path built from *gritstone* blocks. A little way above that, the path climbs a short limestone escarpment. The easiest way when it's wet, is to follow the path right, then to move back to the left, though when dry there are several other options.

The way continues upwards, passing through an area of boulders before climbing through another escarpment, this time *gritstone* instead of limestone.

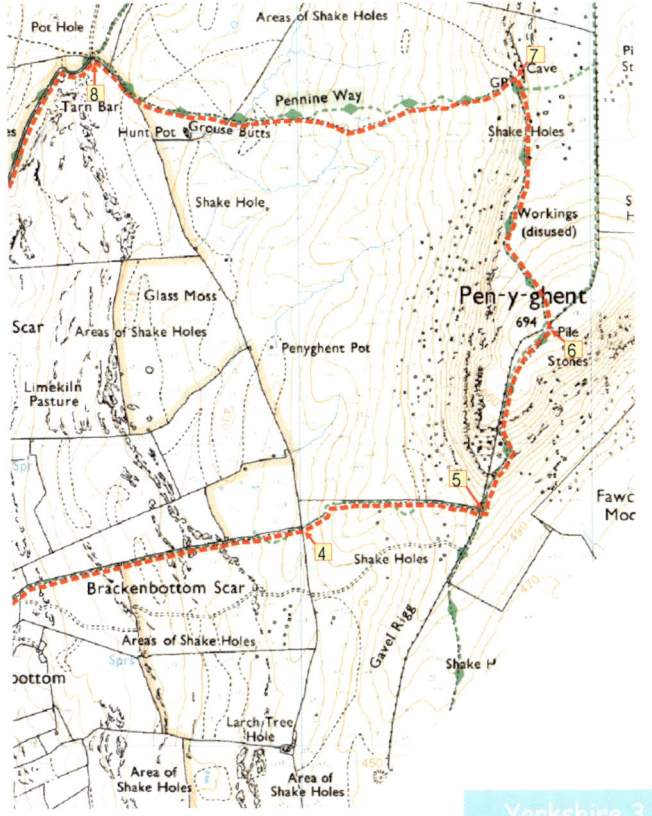

The gritstone escarpment near the summit

There's no great difficulty and the grip of the rock is very reassuring. The path then levels out a bit to continue more easily to the summit (Wp.6 101M) with its *trig point*, walled shelter and two small gate stiles that give access to the other side of the wall, and our return route.

The walled shelter is a good place to linger. The prevailing winds come from the southwest, and if it is at all breezy the strength of the wind isn't appreciated until the wall is crossed to make our descent. In these conditions the hill is well named 'Hill of the Winds'. The nearby sign indicates the route of the **Pennine Way**, and we follow the way indicated (NNW) to 'Horton in Ribblesdale'.

The path is a bit scrappy at first, but soon becomes more distinct as it descends, eventually turning more to the north, then running along the top of the steep western slopes of the mountain. The descent continues that way until it reaches a sharp left turn (Wp.7 133M) next to a large flattened cairn with a much fainter path going straight on. We take the left turn and continue down the good path in a mainly westerly direction.

As the downhill gradient begins to level out we reach a wall with a gate and two wooden ladder stiles. The path then continues to a second wall with gates and stiles, and just beyond that, a junction with a wide track and a gate (Wp.8 161M).

Hull Pot

An optional extra at this point is to visit the dramatic **Hull Pot**, which is only five minutes walk away. We turn right at Wp.8 and follow the obvious grassy path (NNE) for just over 300 metres.

You can't miss **Hull Pot**, because it's enormous. It's also hugely spectacular whatever the weather. When it's fine, look for the dry stream bed on the far (NE) side of the hole. When it rains it becomes a raging torrent, so take your camera whatever the weather. When finished, we return to the gate at Wp.8.

We go through the gate and follow the walled track (SW) and continue that way for half an hour, gradually losing height. The walled track is an old drove road, and navigation doesn't get any easier than this. This gives lots of opportunity for looking around and admiring the scenery, but the sight guaranteed to draw the eye is the magnificent bulk of **Pen y Ghent**, still rising above us on our left.

The descent down Horton Lane

Our descent comes to a fork in the track (Wp.9 192M). The left branch keeps to the same level, but we take the right descending branch, passing through a wooden gate. A short distance on we meet the road that passes through **Horton in Ribblesdale** (Wp.10 197M).

At this point we may have to face the most difficult decision of the day. Turn left to the **Golden Lion** or right to the **Crown**. If you are staying at **Horton** overnight you could do both.

For those who don't want a pint (or two), or have to drive home, the **Pen y Ghent Café** and the car park are both a couple of minutes away to the right.

So, that's it, the first of our walks leading eventually to the Yorkshire Three Peaks Challenge.

2 WHERNSIDE FROM RIBBLEHEAD

Whernside is the highest peak in **Yorkshire** at 736 metres, although it has to share the summit with the neighbouring county of **Cumbria**. We start from **Ribblehead** near to the magnificent **Ribblehead Viaduct**, which carries the **Settle** to **Carlisle** railway line to the east of the hill. We follow the railway for a while until it disappears into the **Blea Moor** tunnel. From there we start gaining height to reach the summit ridge and the top. The descent is straightforward, and we finish by tracing a route along the foot of the hill back to **Ribblehead**, a place with more than its fair share of history. The area round the viaduct was a huge camp for the navvies who built the railway, and the site is of great interest to archaeologists.

It's worth timing the ascent from the start point to the summit, because the next time we pass this way we will use a shortcut that may save time on the day of the Challenge.

| 4 | 4H | 7.8 miles/12.6km | 478m / 478m | | 4 |

Access by car: The start point for the walk is **Ribblehead**, which sits on the junction of the B6255 **Ingleton** to **Hawes** road and the B6479 road, which runs from **Settle** to **Ribblehead**. So, depending on where you are travelling from, **Ribblehead** is approached from **Ingleton**, **Hawes** or **Settle**. There is plenty of parking in lay-bys, though please avoid driving on to any grassed areas, as these are of significant archaeological interest. **Ribblehead** is also on the **Carlisle** to **Settle** rail line, making a car-free trip not only practical, but also positively enjoyable; any waiting time for the train for the return trip can be usefully spent in the **Station Inn**.

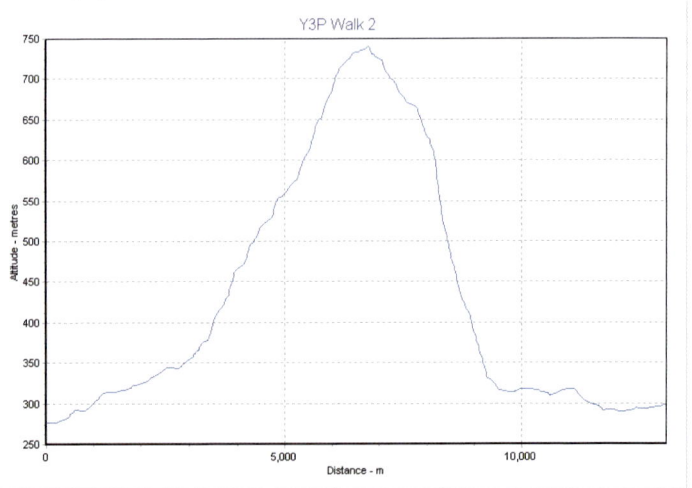

Y3P Walk 2

We start the walk about 50 metres downhill from the **Station Inn** where a track leaves the roadside (Wp.1 0M) heading towards the railway viaduct (NW) with the railway line running parallel on our left. (Don't forget to time how long it takes from here to the summit.)

Our path starts to curve left to head under the viaduct, with a line of boulders on the right hand side of the path (Wp.2 7M). Here we go straight on (wooden signpost to 'Whernside') with the railway still running parallel on our left. We continue like this for just over half an hour, ignoring tracks running under the railway. The second of these, a bridleway, is the route

On the track alongside the viaduct

Crossing one of the streams

of an ancient packhorse route running from **Ingleton** to **Dentdale**. Our path merges with the bridleway and continues in the same direction as before, passing the site of **Blea Moor** station and sidings along the way. The bridleway is always obvious and easy to follow, and crosses a couple of small streams along the way, using stepping-stones and a bridge.

After just over half an hour from **Ribblehead** the bridleway crosses the railway by an impressive stone bridge (Wp.3 41M) that also carries the stream across a very deep railway cutting. To the north the railway enters **Blea Moor** tunnel, and looking south the line points straight towards **Ingleborough**.

Immediately after the bridge, a wooden finger post indicates a path to the right to **Dent Head**, but we continue straight on, following the bridleway towards **Dentdale**.

The next section of the bridleway starts to gain some height, with a stone wall running alongside on the left. The bridleway is paved with stone causeway slabs in places, making the walking drier and easier. As we gain height we get good views of **Force Gill** waterfall to the left. The name has Norse origins, *force* (sometimes *foss*) coming from the Old Norse word *fors* meaning a waterfall, and *gill* coming from *gjel*, meaning a ravine.

Force Gill waterfall

Meanwhile, across to the right, we can see a line of three mounds, obviously man-made. These are ventilation shafts marking the line of the railway tunnel.

A short distance beyond the waterfall we come to a wooden step stile crossing

Yorkshire 3 Peaks

the fence on our left (Wp.4 63M).

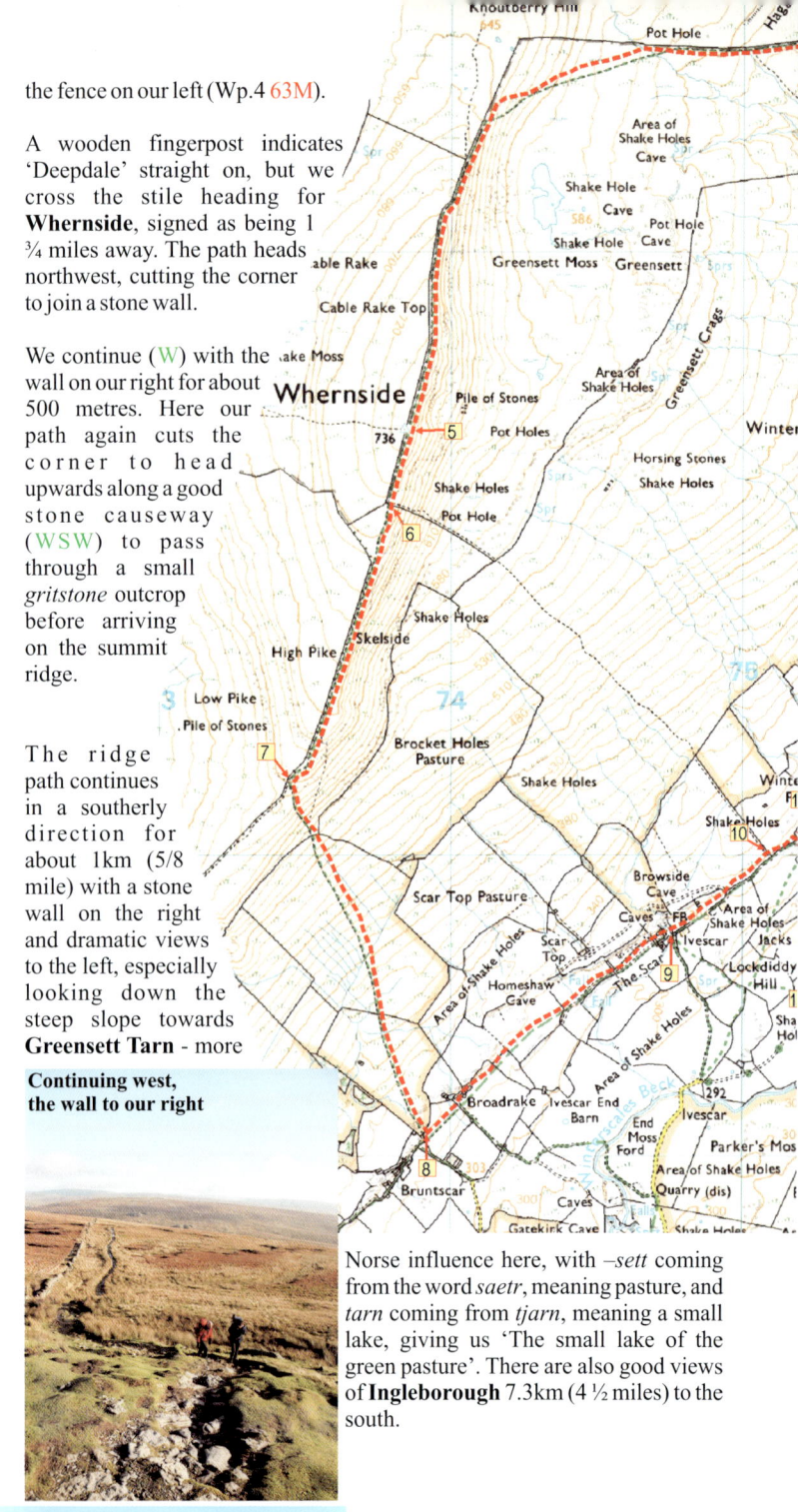

A wooden fingerpost indicates 'Deepdale' straight on, but we cross the stile heading for **Whernside**, signed as being 1 ¾ miles away. The path heads northwest, cutting the corner to join a stone wall.

We continue (W) with the wall on our right for about 500 metres. Here our path again cuts the corner to head upwards along a good stone causeway (WSW) to pass through a small *gritstone* outcrop before arriving on the summit ridge.

The ridge path continues in a southerly direction for about 1km (5/8 mile) with a stone wall on the right and dramatic views to the left, especially looking down the steep slope towards **Greensett Tarn** - more

Continuing west, the wall to our right

Norse influence here, with *–sett* coming from the word *saetr*, meaning pasture, and *tarn* coming from *tjarn*, meaning a small lake, giving us 'The small lake of the green pasture'. There are also good views of **Ingleborough** 7.3km (4 ½ miles) to the south.

44 Yorkshire 3 Peaks

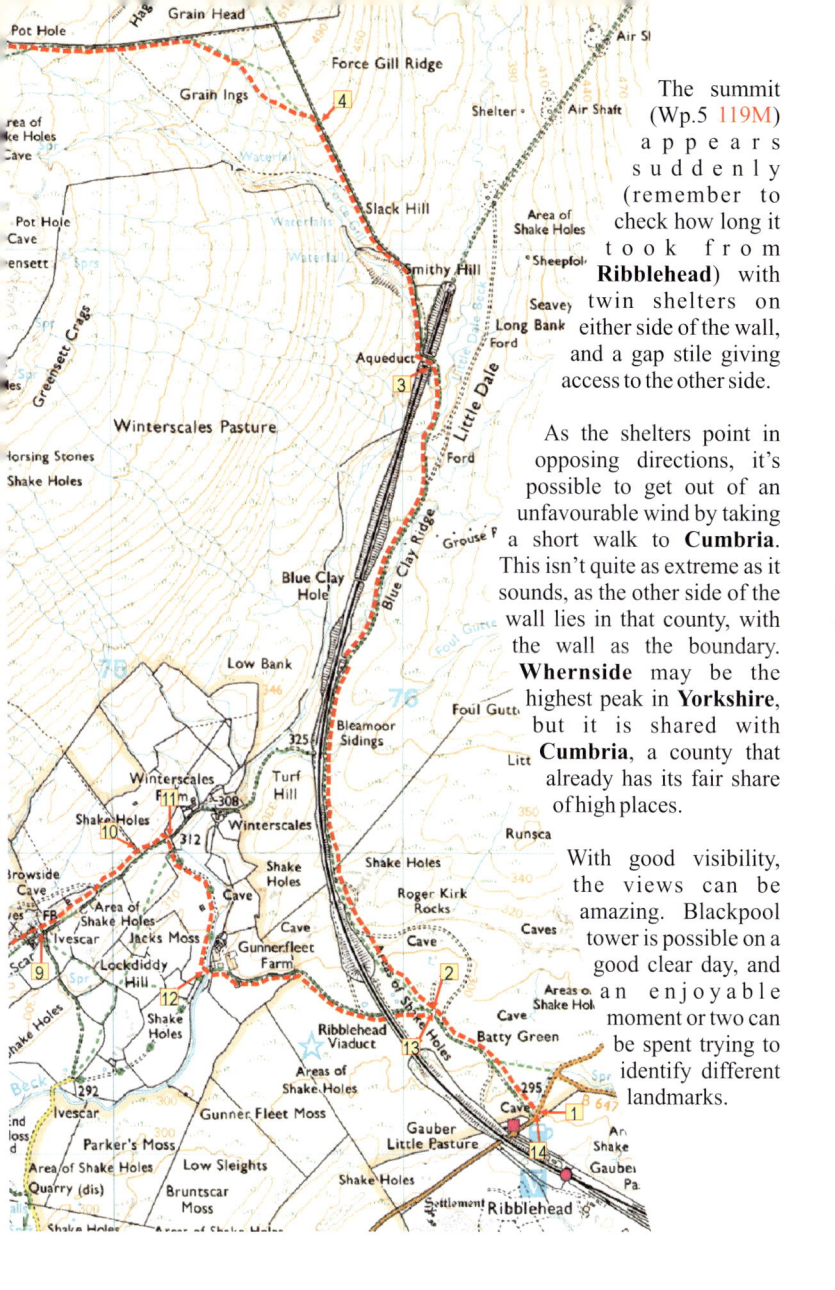

The summit (Wp.5 119M) appears suddenly (remember to check how long it took from **Ribblehead**) with twin shelters on either side of the wall, and a gap stile giving access to the other side.

As the shelters point in opposing directions, it's possible to get out of an unfavourable wind by taking a short walk to **Cumbria**. This isn't quite as extreme as it sounds, as the other side of the wall lies in that county, with the wall as the boundary. **Whernside** may be the highest peak in **Yorkshire**, but it is shared with **Cumbria**, a county that already has its fair share of high places.

With good visibility, the views can be amazing. Blackpool tower is possible on a good clear day, and an enjoyable moment or two can be spent trying to identify different landmarks.

When the time comes to leave we continue in the same direction as before (SSW), but descending now, for about 250 metres to where a fence rises up from the left to a gate which lies across our path (Wp.6 123M). The line of the rising fence is the way we will be coming up when we do Walk 5. That's for another day, though, and today we go through the gate and carry on downwards as before.

Yorkshire 3 Peaks 45

Our path continues descending ...

Our path continues descending (SSW), always easy to follow, for about 1km to where the well defined path suddenly turns to the left heading downhill, and a faint path carries straight on descending next to the wall (Wp.7 143M). We take the well-defined path descending to the left, steep in places, but stone steps give security underfoot.

We cross two stone walls, the first by step stiles, the second by ladder stiles, until the path goes through a gate with a small stone barn on the left. Just beyond the barn, the path comes to a bridleway (Wp.8 189M).

To the right the bridleway is a stony track, but we turn left to go through a gate following a grassy track. This is part of the ancient **Ingleton** to **Dentdale** packhorse route we walked earlier in the day. The grassy way passes the habitation at **Broadrake**, continuing (NE) through several gates for just over 1km to **Ivescar Farm** (Wp.9 209M).

The bridleway at Broadrake

The bridleway continues in the same direction as before (NE) passing through the farm with a long outbuilding on our right. 400 metres beyond the outbuilding we come to a ladder stile on the left (Wp.10 215M).

The ladder stile crosses the wall giving access to the muddy looking path rising (NW) by the wall. This is the outward part of our route for Walk 5, but today we continue along the bridleway for 100 metres to a junction to the right (Wp.11 217M). We take the right junction, and follow the narrow road towards the large farm of **Gunnerfleet**, across the stream on our left. Just beyond **Gunnerfleet** is a junction to the left (Wp.12 223M).

We take the junction to the left, crossing the stream by a bridge. The track continues heading mainly east to pass under one of the arches of the **Ribblehead Viaduct** to join the track on which we started our day (Wp.13 236M). From here we follow the wide track back to the start point by the road (Wp.14 242M). For those waiting for the train, there's no finer place to spend the time than the **Station Inn**. Others not dependent on the railway will still find a warm welcome.

3 INGLEBOROUGH FROM THE HILL INN

Ingleborough is the most distinctive of the Three Peaks, the one that is iconic of Yorkshire Dales scenery - and instantly recognisable. We start from **The Hill Inn** at **Chapel le Dale** and follow old paths towards the vast bog of Humphrey Bottom. Fortunately we can cross this dry shod using a stone causeway, which takes us to a steep ascent to the *col* between **Simon Fell** and **Ingleborough**. From there a short but easy scramble takes us to the summit, with a vast panorama which, on a good day, stretches from the Lake District fells to Snowdonia. You won't be the first on **Ingleborough** by a long way. The Romans had a military camp here, and the Brigantes were here before them.

On the early part of the walk

We could retrace our steps by the ascent route, but a more interesting way is to follow a terrace around the slopes of **Simon Fell** to descend by **Park Fell**, giving excellent views of **Pen y Ghent** and **Whernside** and the route connecting them.

4 | 4H | 7.9 miles/12.8km | 513m / 513m | 4

Access by car: The start point is at **Chapel le Dale** between **Ingleton** and **Ribblehead** on the B6255. 250 metres uphill (NE) of the **Hill Inn** is a lay-by with room for several cars (this can soon fill up in summer, so don't be late) The walk start point (Wp.1 0M) is between the lay-by and the **Hill Inn**, and is signed to 'Great Douk' and 'Ingleborough'.

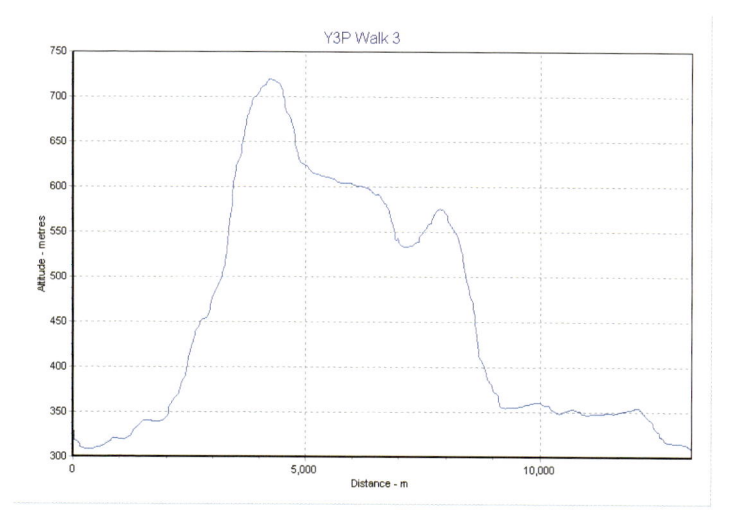

Y3P Walk 3

Yorkshire 3 Peaks 47

The panel at the start

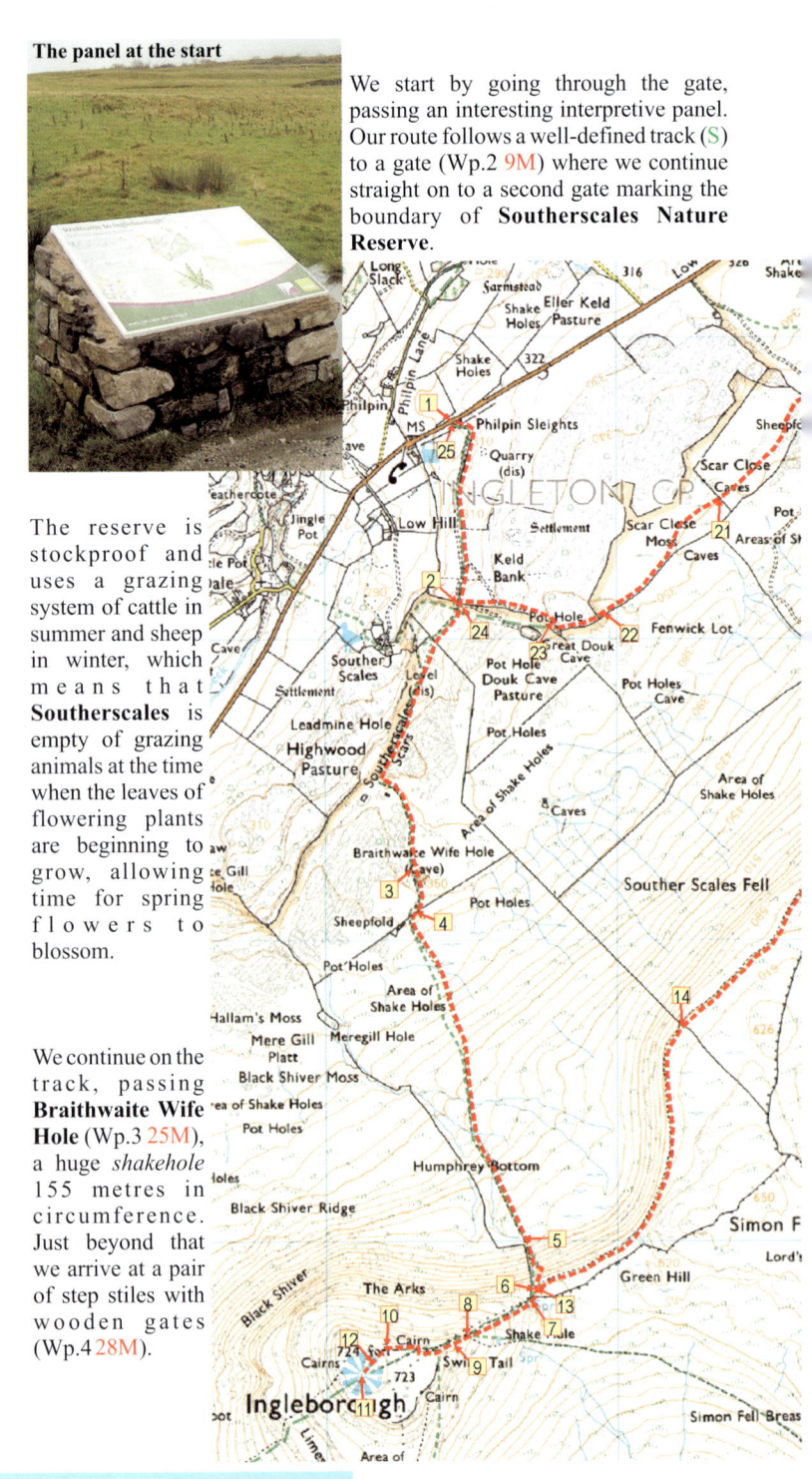

We start by going through the gate, passing an interesting interpretive panel. Our route follows a well-defined track (S) to a gate (Wp.2 9M) where we continue straight on to a second gate marking the boundary of **Southerscales Nature Reserve**.

The reserve is stockproof and uses a grazing system of cattle in summer and sheep in winter, which means that **Southerscales** is empty of grazing animals at the time when the leaves of flowering plants are beginning to grow, allowing time for spring flowers to blossom.

We continue on the track, passing **Braithwaite Wife Hole** (Wp.3 25M), a huge *shakehole* 155 metres in circumference. Just beyond that we arrive at a pair of step stiles with wooden gates (Wp.4 28M).

48 Yorkshire 3 Peaks

After crossing the stone wall using one of the twin stiles, we continue across the vast bog of **Humphrey Bottom** (no sniggering at the back, please!). Fortunately we can cross this dry shod by means of a stone causeway; although such improvements are sometimes controversial, this path was a mire about 50 metres wide before its construction and it prevents erosion, making walking more of a pleasure. What's more, similar causeways have been used in parts of Yorkshire for centuries, so they're far from being a new idea.

The causeway path

The path at Wp.6 after heavy rain

After 20 minutes easy walking while gradually gaining height, we come to a sudden steepening in the path (Wp.5 50M). Here the path suddenly leaps up the hillside, gaining almost 100 metres in height. The route is a set of well constructed steps, and steady progress brings us to a point where our path crosses a small beck (Wp.6 62M).

30 metres beyond the beck crossing we pass through a wooden gate (Wp.7) before continuing on the paved path (WSW) gaining height as we go. About 250 metres beyond the gate another paved

Yorkshire 3 Peaks 49

path joins us from the left (Wp.8). This is the path we'll use when we do the Challenge route to descend to **Horton in Ribblesdale**.

On the summit plateau at Wp.9

Our way continues rising for another 75 metres, through a short section of crag, to the summit plateau (Wp.9 75M). (It's worth remembering this point if it's misty, as the summit plateau can be very confusing in poor visibility.) Follow the gently rising path on the edge of the summit plateau (W) for a little less than 200 metres to where it starts to descend slightly (Wp.10).

From there, head (SW) straight for the *trig point* (Wp.11) to claim your summit. The adjacent cross shaped shelter (Wp.12 80M) makes a good spot for a welcome break.

From here we could follow the way of ascent back to the **Hill Inn**, but a better way is to go for a detour along the side of **Simon Fell** then **Park Fell**. From the summit we retrace our steps along the edge of the summit plateau then down the paved path to the beck we crossed on the way up (Wp.13 92M). On the other side of the beck we take the level path (ENE) instead of the way we used coming up.

Looking back to Ingleborough from the terrace

This path follows a level terrace near to the 600 metre contour, giving great walking and absolutely fabulous views, especially back towards **Ingleborough** and across the dale to **Whernside**. The terrace path meets a wall with a step stile (Wp.14) then starts to descend the broad north ridge of **Simon Fell**.

The path levels out as a wall joins our route from the right (Wp.15). We continue with the wall on our right, gaining height slightly on the flank of **Park Fell**, crossing a dilapidated wooden step stile on the way. The path soon turns to head east briefly before arriving at a T-junction of walls (Wp.16 136M).

At the T-junction a small marker post indicates straight on to a wooden step stile, but we turn left and descend the steep slopes of **Park Fell** (NE) following the wall on our right - the path is well defined. The views across to **Pen y Ghent** on one side, and the **Ribblehead Viaduct** on the other are superb. At the bottom of the steep bit we cross the stone wall using the step stile (Wp.17) then continue with the wall still on our right towards the

50 Yorkshire 3 Peaks

buildings at **Colt Park**. Just before **Colt Park** we reach a wooden finger post (Wp.18 154M). Our route turns to the left in the direction indicated (WNW) and follows the narrow grassy path, crossing a step stile then passing through two wooden gates in succession. At the second gate (Wp.19 172M) our route turns to the left and follows the wall on our left to a gate, also on the left (Wp.20 181M). We don't take this gate, but instead go through the other nearby gate about 50 metres away, ahead and to the right.

The path continues in roughly the same direction as before (SW) to yet another gate (Wp.21). We go through this and continue straight on as before, occasional small posts with blue markers confirming the route. The path gradually drifts left to meet a wall running parallel and on the left. We follow this to a substantial wooden gate (Wp.22 202M), which we use to get to the other side of the wall.

Following the wall (now on our right) for about 150 metres, brings us to another gate, giving access to a small enclosure, with a small gate on the left and a wider gate at the far end (Wp.23).

The small gate leads to **Great Douk Cave**, but our way goes through the wider gate, and turns immediately left and follows the wall on the left to a gate and the path we started on (Wp.24 220M). Here we turn right and head back to the start point (Wp.25 227M). To the right is the parking at the lay-by, but beckoning to the left is the **Hill Inn**, a good place to end the walk.

THE MISSING LINKS - FILLING IN THE GAPS

Whernside in the afternoon

The challenge of completing the Three Peaks in one walk wouldn't be anything like as difficult if they were all moved closer to each other. As this isn't an option, we have to find the most efficient ways to link the Peaks together. These walks are the missing pieces of the jigsaw puzzle that makes up the circuit. They also make interesting walks in their own right, and will give an idea of what it is like to complete the challenge.

The Three Peaks Challenge route splits naturally into three sections - **Horton in Ribblesdale** to **Ribblehead** via **Pen y Ghent**, **Ribblehead** to the **Hill Inn** via **Whernside** and the **Hill Inn** to **Horton in Ribblesdale** via **Ingleborough**. The next three walks cover all the ground we need to know for the big day itself.

4 HORTON IN RIBBLESDALE, PEN Y GHENT, RIBBLEHEAD

This first leg of the Challenge route retraces the route we took up **Pen y Ghent** from **Horton in Ribblesdale**. However, the descent doesn't take us back to the welcoming pubs and cafes of **Horton in Ribblesdale** as before. Instead we set off across country before joining a section of the **Pennine Way.** If any part of the Challenge route requires care in navigation, this is it! It's also physically and psychologically demanding, being the longest of the three sections of the Challenge. It's a case of "steady away" as they say up north, and bit by bit the **Ribblehead Viaduct** gets nearer and nearer, marking the end of today's efforts. The section of the route between Wps.7&11 became the 'Approved' Y3P route in 2013, replacing what used to be the dismal trudge through the bogs of T**odber Moss** and **Red Moss**. In places it has been signed 'Yorkshire Three Peaks High Birkwith via Whitber'; path improvements are currently being made, making the route easier to follow.

5 5½H 10.25 miles/16.5km 647m / 587m 4

Access by car: This is a linear walk starting at **Horton in Ribblesdale** (for travel directions by car see Walk 1) and finishing at **Ribblehead**. The easiest solution for transport logistics is to park a car at **Ribblehead** (see Walk 2) then to drive in a second car to the start point in **Horton**. If two cars are not available there are trains about every two hours to complete the link. In this case drive to **Ribblehead**, park up and take the train to **Horton,** starting the walk at the railway station. This way you walk back to your car without any time pressure to catch a train at the end of the day.

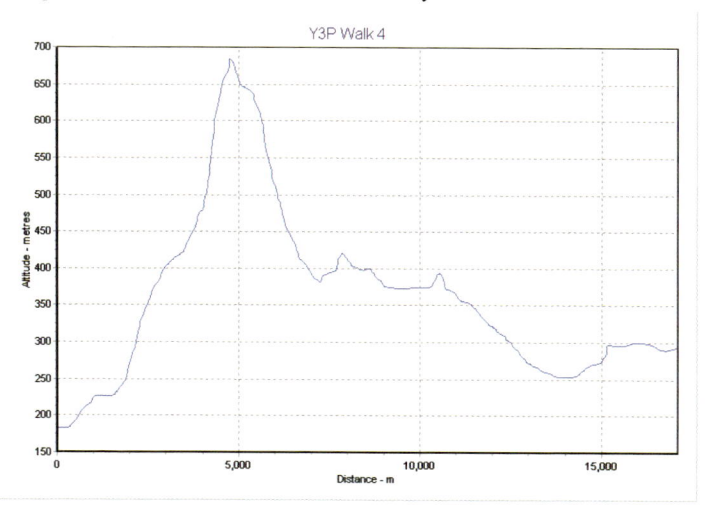

Y3P Walk 4

The start point is the car park in **Horton** (Wp.1 0M) so train users have to walk down the hill towards the village, crossing over the footbridge near the Crown Inn, an extra 5 minutes walk in all. As before we head towards **Settle**, passing the **Pen y Ghent Café**, the **Golden Lion**, and **St Oswald's** church. After the church we take the second minor road on the left (Wp.2 8M). Our route

Yorkshire 3 Peaks 53

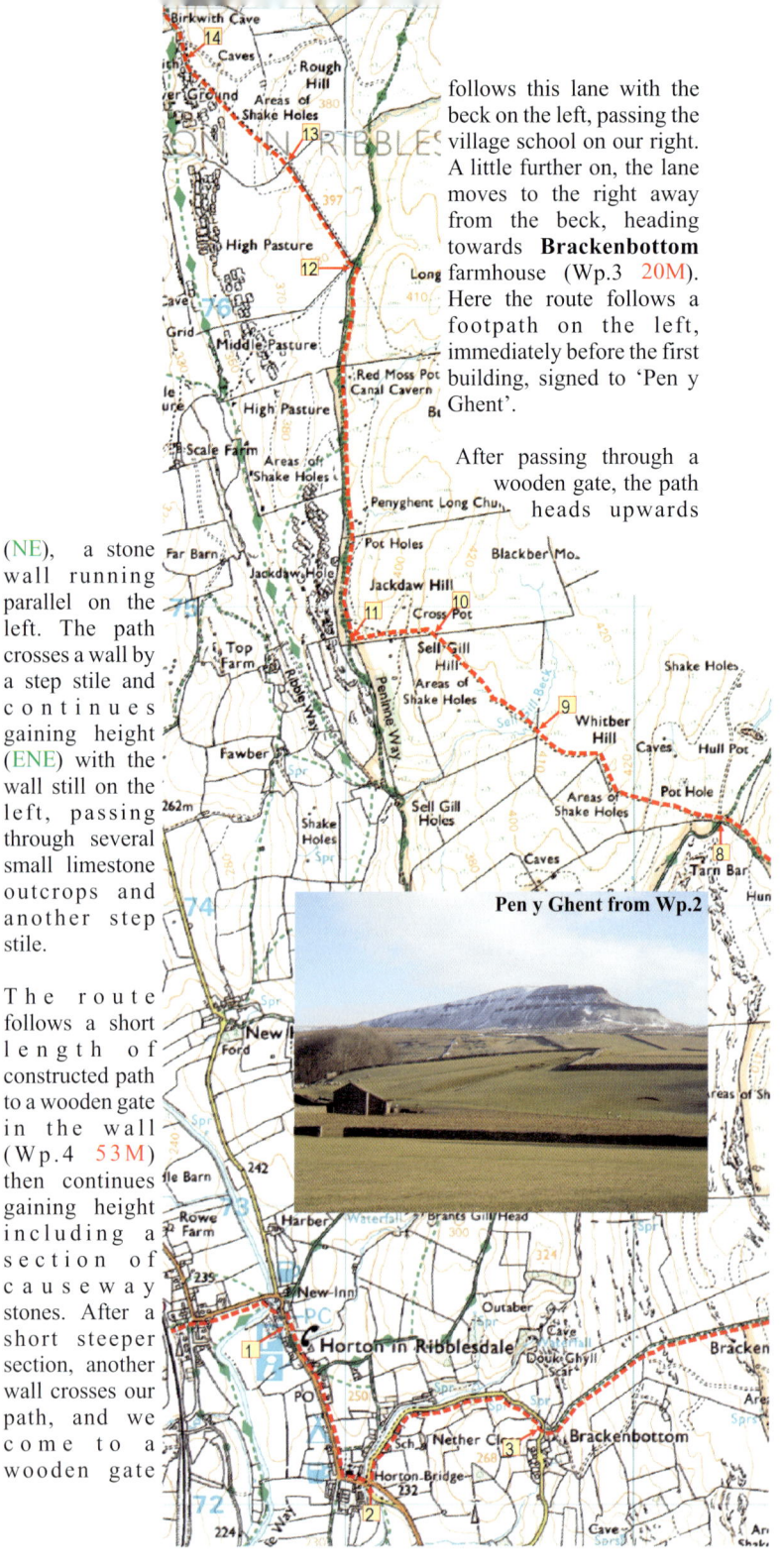

follows this lane with the beck on the left, passing the village school on our right. A little further on, the lane moves to the right away from the beck, heading towards **Brackenbottom** farmhouse (Wp.3 20M). Here the route follows a footpath on the left, immediately before the first building, signed to 'Pen y Ghent'.

After passing through a wooden gate, the path heads upwards (NE), a stone wall running parallel on the left. The path crosses a wall by a step stile and continues gaining height (ENE) with the wall still on the left, passing through several small limestone outcrops and another step stile.

The route follows a short length of constructed path to a wooden gate in the wall (Wp.4 53M) then continues gaining height including a section of causeway stones. After a short steeper section, another wall crosses our path, and we come to a wooden gate

Pen y Ghent from Wp.2

(Wp.5 72M) where we join the **Pennine Way**. Here we turn left and continue upwards on a well-constructed path built from *gritstone* blocks. A little way above that, the path climbs a short limestone escarpment where there are several route options. The way continues upwards, passing through an area of boulders before climbing through another escarpment, this time *gritstone* instead of limestone. The path then levels out to continue more easily to the summit (Wp.6 101M) with its *trig point*, walled shelter and two small gate stiles giving us access to the other side of the wall.

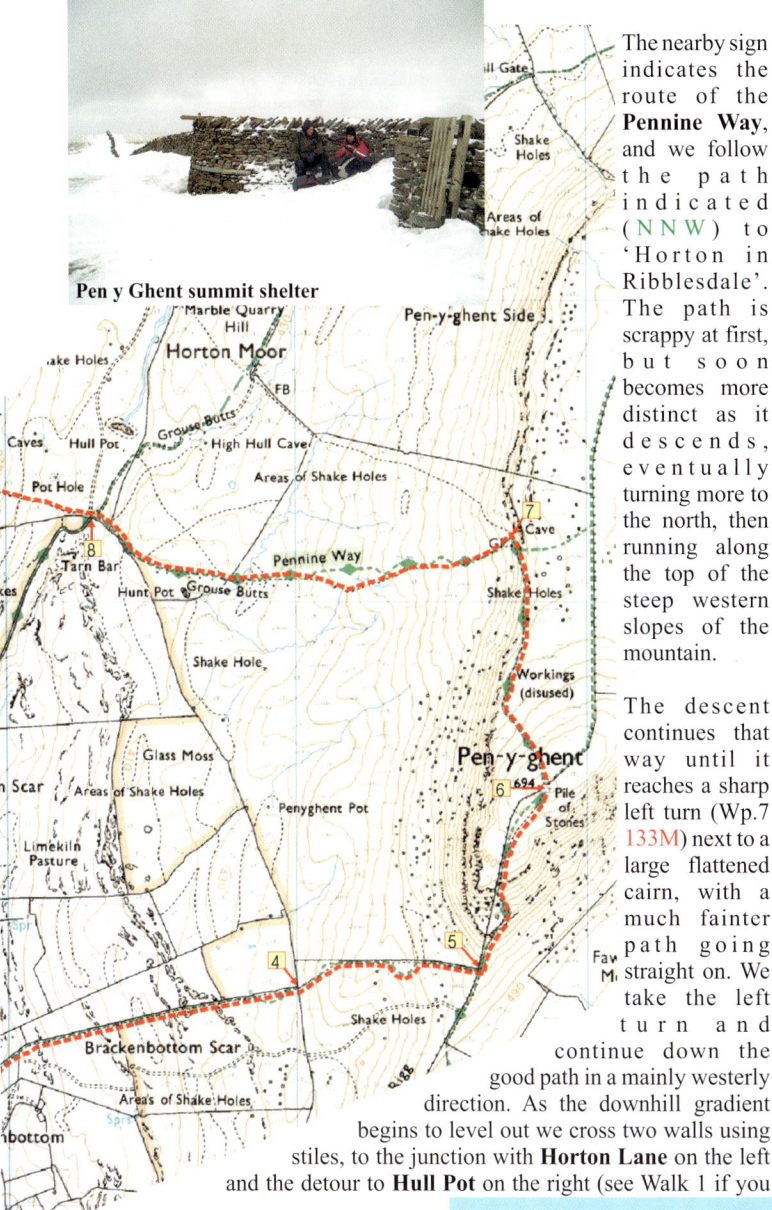

Pen y Ghent summit shelter

The nearby sign indicates the route of the **Pennine Way**, and we follow the path indicated (NNW) to 'Horton in Ribblesdale'. The path is scrappy at first, but soon becomes more distinct as it descends, eventually turning more to the north, then running along the top of the steep western slopes of the mountain.

The descent continues that way until it reaches a sharp left turn (Wp.7 133M) next to a large flattened cairn, with a much fainter path going straight on. We take the left turn and continue down the good path in a mainly westerly direction. As the downhill gradient begins to level out we cross two walls using stiles, to the junction with **Horton Lane** on the left and the detour to **Hull Pot** on the right (see Walk 1 if you

Yorkshire 3 Peaks 55

missed this last time) (Wp.8 161M).

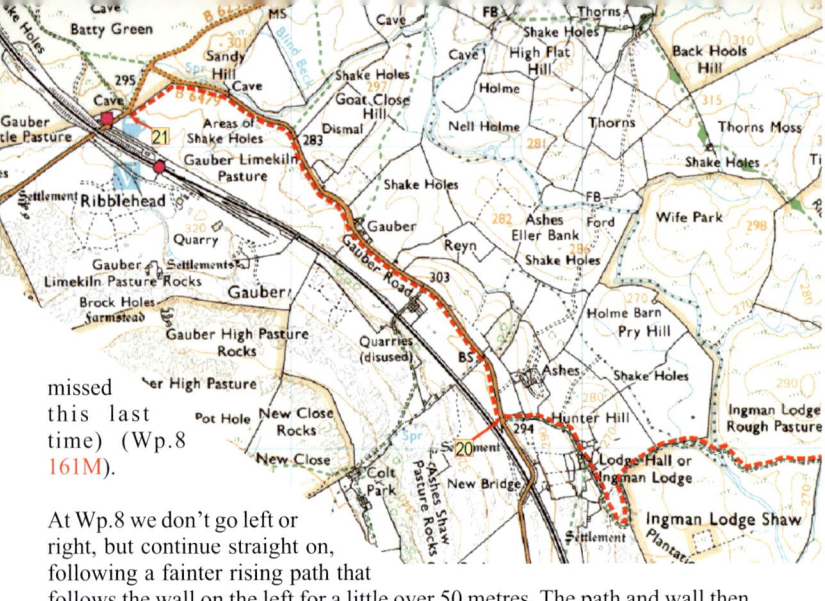

At Wp.8 we don't go left or right, but continue straight on, following a fainter rising path that follows the wall on the left for a little over 50 metres. The path and wall then start to diverge, but after 300 metres they come back together again. At this point we turn right and walk with the wall on our left. In just over 100 metres the wall on the left comes to a right angle corner to the left.

The gate at Wp.9

The path appears to go straight on, but the path we need is the fainter one to the left, which gradually drifts away rightwards from the stone wall. After 200 metres this path descends gradually to a wooden gate next to a ramshackle stone wall (Wp.9 177M). We go through the gate, with one wall going diagonally left and the other one diagonally right.

We follow a faint sunken path that splits the angle of the two walls, crossing **Sell Gill Beck** almost immediately. The path becomes so faint that it disappears, but we continue in the same general direction (NW) over boggy ground towards a stone wall that runs across our line of travel. As the wall gets nearer there's an obvious gate to head for (Wp.10 186M); we go through the gate and turn left to follow the wall downhill for almost 300 metres to a wide grassy track crossing our path (Wp.11 194M). This is the **Pennine Way**, and it goes through a gate in the wall we've been following on our left. We don't go left though; instead we turn right (N) and follow the **Pennine Way** for about twenty minutes with a stone wall on our left, passing through two stone walls along the way.

About five minutes after passing through the second wall we need to keep a lookout for a step stile (Wp.12 216M) crossing the wall on our left. Before crossing the stile if we look back to the right we will see the traditional Three

56   Yorkshire 3 Peaks

The step stile at Wp.12

peaks route joining us, coming from the direction of the mires of **Todber Moss** and **Red Moss**.

Once over the stile we are back on the original route, heading NNW. The next short section can be boggy, but is heaven compared with the traditional **Todber Moss** route that we've avoided. The path climbs slightly before descending gently to a slot stile in a wall (Wp.13 225M) From there we continue following the path (NW) which becomes fainter, but still discernible, heading towards an large area of what appears at first to be limestone blocks, but which is a section of *limestone pavement*. We keep this on our left, and join a farm track coming from our right (Wp.14 236M).

.. our path goes *across* this track (Wp.15)

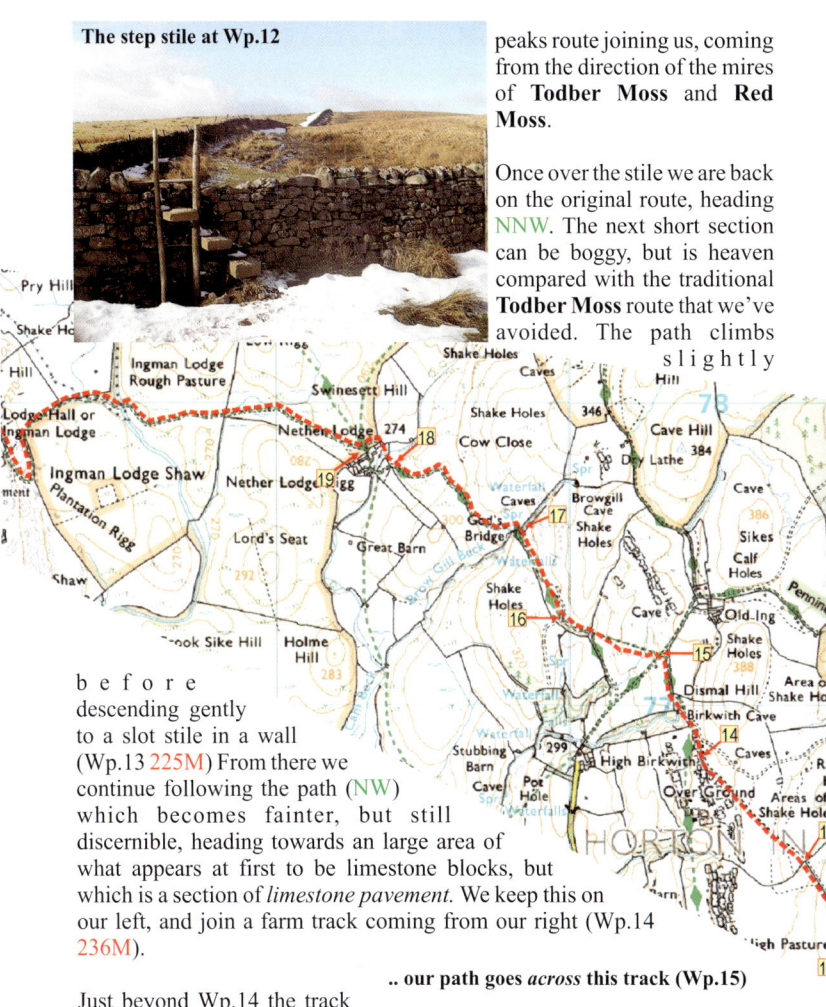

Just beyond Wp.14 the track passes a walled area on the left with trees and a deep cut ravine - this is **Birkwith Cave**. The track then comes to a gate with a slot stile next to it. Beyond there we continue on the track with a stone wall on our right, to a junction with a wider track (Wp.15 240M) running across our line of travel.

Our path goes *across* this track, and drops into the shallow gully ahead, with a wooden railway sleeper bridge crossing the narrow beck. We follow the fading path (WNW) gently gaining height before dropping down to a gate with a good track on the other side. We go through the gate and follow the

Yorkshire 3 Peaks 57

track for about 100 metres. Here the track suddenly turns uphill to the right, next to a large limestone block and a wooden fingerpost (Wp.16 247M) but we go straight on, following the wall on our left. The path goes through a gap between converging stone walls, to a gate (Wp.17 254M)

.. straight on following the wall on our left (Wp.16)

The footbridge at Nether Lodge (Wp.18)

just above **God's Bridge**, a natural limestone bridge over **Brow Gill Beck**. We follow the good footpath that widens into a track heading to the buildings at **Nether Lodge**. Here we head to the right of the house, crossing a footbridge (Wp.18 265M)

The track to Ribblehead

over **Ling Gill Beck**.

Beyond the bridge we go through the wooden gate and turn left, with the buildings on our left, and head for the obvious track with a finger post (Wp.19 270M).

Lodge Hall

We follow the wide obvious track, initially heading WNW towards **Ribblehead**, for 2km, allowing good progress, passing the impressive **Lodge Hall** (1687), shortly before reaching the B6479 road (Wp.20 295M). Here we go right along the road to **Ribblehead**.

Road walking isn't much fun, but it is the most direct way to **Ribblehead**. The road can be busy, but the bends keep the speed of the traffic down; remember to walk on the right, facing the oncoming traffic. Just less than 2km later we arrive at **Ribblehead** (Wp.21 323M) where we can celebrate finishing the first section of the Three Peaks Challenge in the **Station Inn**. Before going in, take a good look at **Whernside** looming ahead - that's next on our list.

58 Yorkshire 3 Peaks

5 RIBBLEHEAD, WHERNSIDE, HILL INN

The second leg of the challenge starts from **Ribblehead** but instead of following the railway as on Walk 2, we follow the old Three Peaks Challenge route starting near **Winterscales Farm**. There's only one way to describe the ascent – unremittingly steep! It's so steep that a descent would not be pleasant. Going up isn't a lot of fun either, but it is over 2.5 kms shorter, and could save up to 40 minutes. Time the ascent and compare it with your time for Walk 2 Whernside from Ribblehead, and pick your route for the big day accordingly. If the ascent is daunting, the way down is straightforward, following the way we took last time. This time, though, we carry on down to the road at the **Hill Inn**, thereby completing the second leg of the Challenge route. From the inn, it's a steady walk back to **Ribblehead**.

4 | 4H | 7.9 miles 12.5km | 528m / 528m | 4

Access by car: The start point for the walk is **Ribblehead**, which sits on the junction of the B6255 **Ingleton** to **Hawes** road and the B6479 road, which runs from **Settle** to **Ribblehead**. So, depending on where you are travelling from, **Ribblehead** is approached from **Ingleton**, **Hawes** or **Settle**. Although there's plenty of parking in lay-bys, please avoid driving on to any grassed areas, as these are of significant archaeological interest. **Ribblehead** is also on the **Carlisle** to **Settle** rail line, making a car-free trip not only practical, but positively enjoyable; any waiting time for the train for the return trip can be usefully spent in the **Station Inn**.

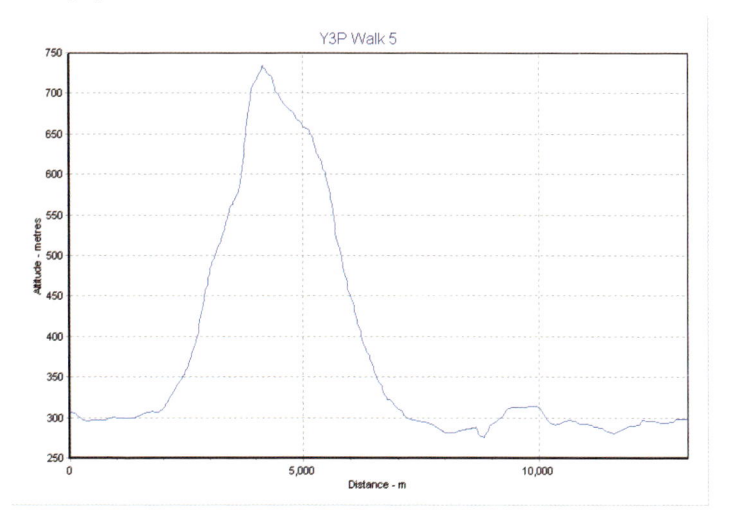

We start the walk from the same place as in Walk 2, about 50 metres downhill from the **Station Inn** where a track leaves the roadside (Wp.1 0M) heading towards the railway viaduct (NW) with the railway line running parallel on the left. (Don't forget to time how long it takes you from here to the summit) After 500 metres the path starts to curve left to head under the viaduct, with a line of boulders on the right hand side of the path (Wp.2 7M).

Instead of going straight on as we did on Walk 2, we follow the track as it bends left to pass under **Ribblehead Viaduct**. Easy walking on the broad track brings us to a bridge over **Winterscales Beck** with **Gunnerfleet Farm** on our right. Just over the bridge our track joins another track at a T-junction (Wp.3 15M). More Norse names here – *scales* comes from *skali* and means a summer dwelling, or pasture and *Gunnar* is a man's name. The word fleet, however, is probably from the old English word *flet*, meaning floor. This word has long been used as meaning "house and home"; so we have "Gunnar's house".

At Wp.3 we turn right towards **Winterscales Farm**. After passing through a gate we arrive at another T-junction (Wp.4 22M) where we turn left and follow the track (SW) for 100 metres to a ladder stile crossing the wall on our right (Wp.5 24M).

We cross the wall using the stile, and follow the grassy path heading upwards (NW) with a stone wall on the right. A second ladder stile follows and the path continues still climbing steeply in the same direction.

Just less than 1km beyond the second stile the path comes to a wall corner. We

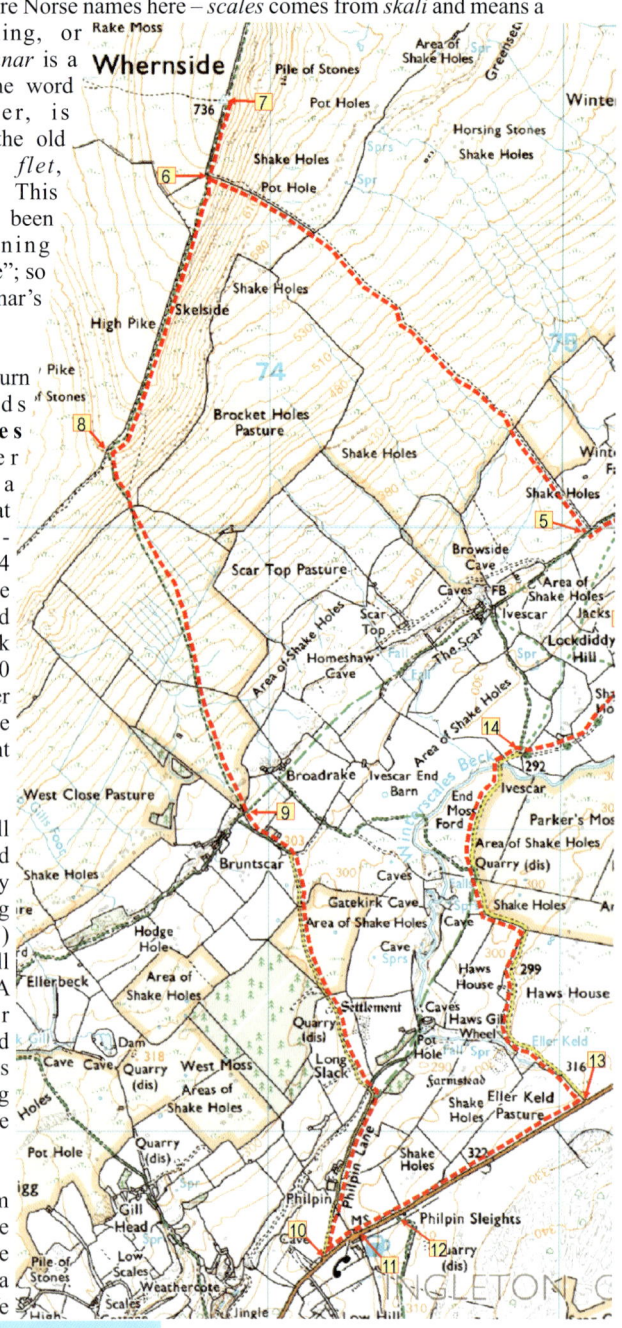

60 Yorkshire 3 Peaks

.. the path suddenly becomes much steeper ..

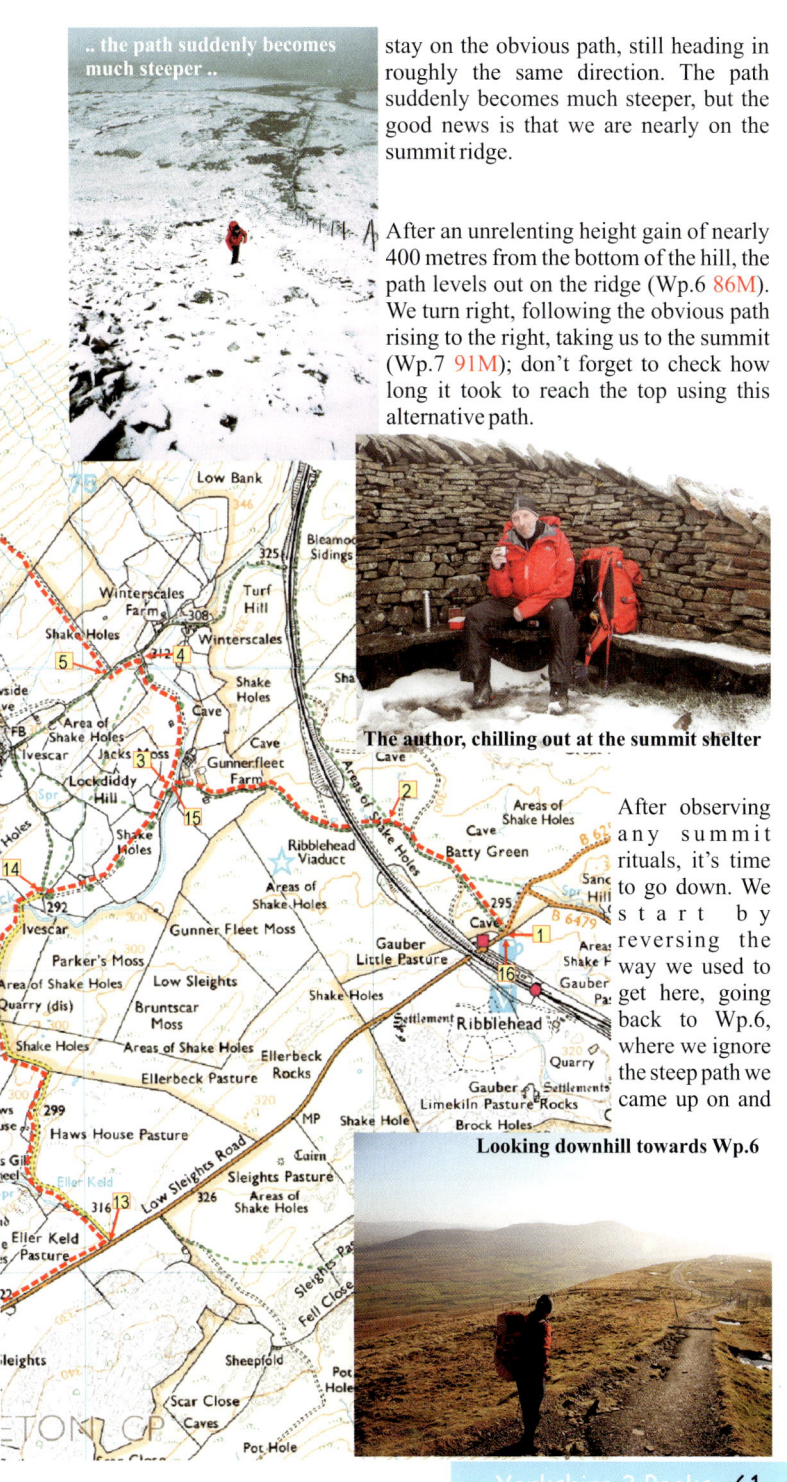

stay on the obvious path, still heading in roughly the same direction. The path suddenly becomes much steeper, but the good news is that we are nearly on the summit ridge.

After an unrelenting height gain of nearly 400 metres from the bottom of the hill, the path levels out on the ridge (Wp.6 86M). We turn right, following the obvious path rising to the right, taking us to the summit (Wp.7 91M); don't forget to check how long it took to reach the top using this alternative path.

The author, chilling out at the summit shelter

After observing any summit rituals, it's time to go down. We start by reversing the way we used to get here, going back to Wp.6, where we ignore the steep path we came up on and

Looking downhill towards Wp.6

Yorkshire 3 Peaks 61

pass through the gate in front of us. As on Walk 2, our path continues descending (SSW) for about 1km to where the well defined path suddenly turns to the left heading downhill, and a faint path carries straight on descending next to the wall (Wp.8 115M).

.. stone steps give security ..

We take the well-defined path descending to the left. The path is steep in places, but as before the stone steps give security underfoot. We cross two stone walls, the first by step stiles, the second by ladder stiles, until the path goes through a gate with a small stone barn on the left.

The descent path towards the Hill Inn

Just beyond the barn, the path comes to a T-junction with a bridleway (Wp.9 161M).

On the bridleway we turn right. In 30 metres we come to a junction to the left, where someone has obligingly fastened a blue road sign with white arrow to the stone wall, confirming that we're on the '3 Peaks Walk'. From here we follow the track then tarmac lane, descending gently in a southerly direction for about 1 km. The lane turns to the right and climbs a little to **Philpin Farm**, where you might be able to buy refreshments in summer. From there, carry on down the lane to meet the **Ingleton** to **Hawes** road (Wp.10 180M).

The Hill Inn, Ingleborough in the background

We turn left and walk up the road for a little over 100 metres to the **Hill Inn** (Wp.11 183M). If you've timed things right, this should make a welcome break at what is a most welcoming pub in every respect.

From here we have a short stretch of road to walk; normally road walking is to be avoided, but to link up this section of the Three Peaks Challenge we have to walk up the road (NE) for almost 200 metres to a gate on the right (Wp.12 185M) with a small water works building just beyond. You may recognise this as the start point for Walk 3, Ingleborough, from the Hill Inn.

62 Yorkshire 3 Peaks

Whernside, above our return route

The next time we come here we'll be doing Walk 6, Ribblehead, Hill Inn, Ingleborough, Horton, but today we carry on up the road (NE) heading towards **Ribblehead**. After 750 metres we come to a narrow tarmac lane off to the left (Wp.13 193M).

We follow this lane for a little over 1 km to where the lane crosses a bridge over the beck. Just beyond the bridge, the lane comes to a Y-fork (Wp.14 209M).

Late afternoon sun on the Ribblehead Viaduct

We take the right fork and follow the track through a gate heading towards **Ribblehead Viaduct.** Approaching the farm, we see the bridge we crossed earlier in the day on our outward leg of the walk as Wp.3 (Wp.15 216M).

We cross the bridge and reverse our earlier route, to bring us back to our start point (Wp.16 233M) at **Ribblehead**. As with Walk 2, a good place to end the walk is in the **Station Inn**.

Whilst sampling the hospitality, this is a good time to compare the times taken on the two different ways to the summit of **Whernside**, and to have a team talk about the route to take on the day of the Three Peaks Challenge. On Walk 2 we took the easier angled but longer route, and today was the shorter distance but with the steep and less pleasant ascent.

The steep way may save crucial time on the day of the Challenge walk, but if completing the walk in less than twelve hours is not an issue, or if your times for the other walks are well within the time required, you may decide to take the more attractive but longer route via **Blea Moor**. Perhaps another pint of the excellent hand-pulled beer at the **Station Inn** will make it all clearer!

6 RIBBLEHEAD, THE HILL INN, INGLEBOROUGH, HORTON IN RIBBLESDALE

This is the last of the training walks before tackling the Challenge route. The aim is to walk the final link route covering the section from the **Hill Inn,** crossing over **Ingleborough** then finishing at **Horton in Ribblesdale**. However, instead of starting the walk from the **Hill Inn**, we start instead from **Ribblehead**. The main advantage of this is that the walk, although linear, can be done without using cars by taking the train from **Horton** to **Ribblehead**. From there we take a section of Walk 5 in reverse to join the third leg of the Challenge at the **Hill Inn**. We then follow the route we followed previously on Walk 3 to the summit of **Ingleborough**, and from there it's a steady descent to the southeast, taking us back to **Horton in Ribblesdale**.

Access by car:
This is another linear route, so the easiest option is to take the train from **Horton in Ribblesdale** to **Ribblehead**, and to follow the easy walk from there to the **Hill Inn** to join the Challenge route. If you are staying in **Horton** for the weekend, it's a short stroll to the railway station from any part of the village. Alternatively you could use two cars, leaving one at **Ribblehead** to collect later or you could even leave a car at the lay-by near the **Hill Inn**, thereby cutting out the 50 minute walk to the **Hill Inn** - but it's all training and gives us the chance to warm up the legs before starting up **Ingleborough**.

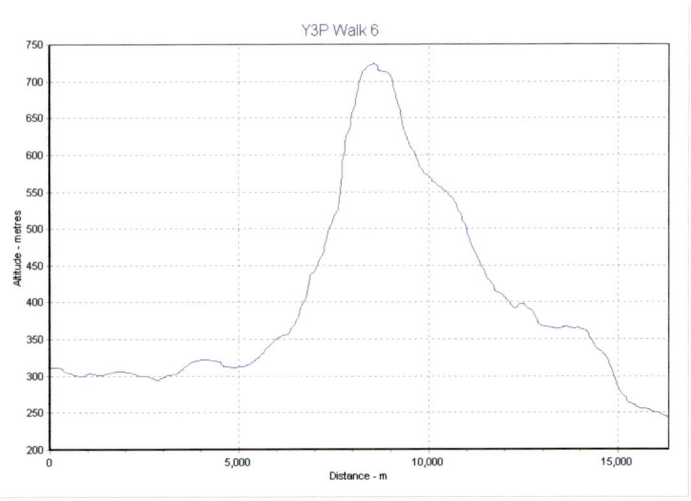

Our start point is the same as in Walk 2 and Walk 5, about 50 metres downhill from the **Station Inn** (Wp.1 0M). We head towards the railway viaduct as before, to where the path starts to curve left to head under the viaduct, with a line of boulders on the right hand side of the path (Wp.2 6M). From there, the route heads under the viaduct and follows the track to the bridge next to

Gunnerfleet Farm.

We cross the bridge over the beck to the T-junction (Wp.3 15M), where we turn left and follow the surfaced track through two gates to a junction with another track (Wp.4 23M).

The minor road heading towards Ingleborough

We then continue straight ahead, crossing over the stream by the bridge, to follow the minor road to the junction with the **Ingleton** to **Ribblehead** road (Wp.5 40M). Here we turn right and walk down the road towards **Ingleton**, remembering to keep to the right hand side, facing the oncoming traffic.

Runners near Ingleborough

After about 8 minutes we arrive at a small concrete waterworks building on the left, just before a field gate, also on the left (Wp.6 48M) which was our start point for Walk 3. We go through the gate, passing the interpretive panel, with a sign for 'Great Douk and Ingleborough', and

.. a pair of step stiles with gates ..

following the same track as on Walk 3 through three gates in succession, the third gate being the entrance to **Southerscales Nature Reserve**. Just past the huge *shakehole* of **Braithwaite Wife Hole** on our left, we reach a pair of step stiles with gates (Wp.7 79M) with a causeway path beyond on the

The final steep ascent

other side of the wall.

The causeway path climbs steadily, eventually levelling out in a dip just below where the path suddenly steepens (Wp.8 102M). A set of well-constructed steps climbs the steep bit, and as this section levels out we cross the stream where the path goes left to

Yorkshire 3 Peaks 65

Inglebrorough trig point and shelter

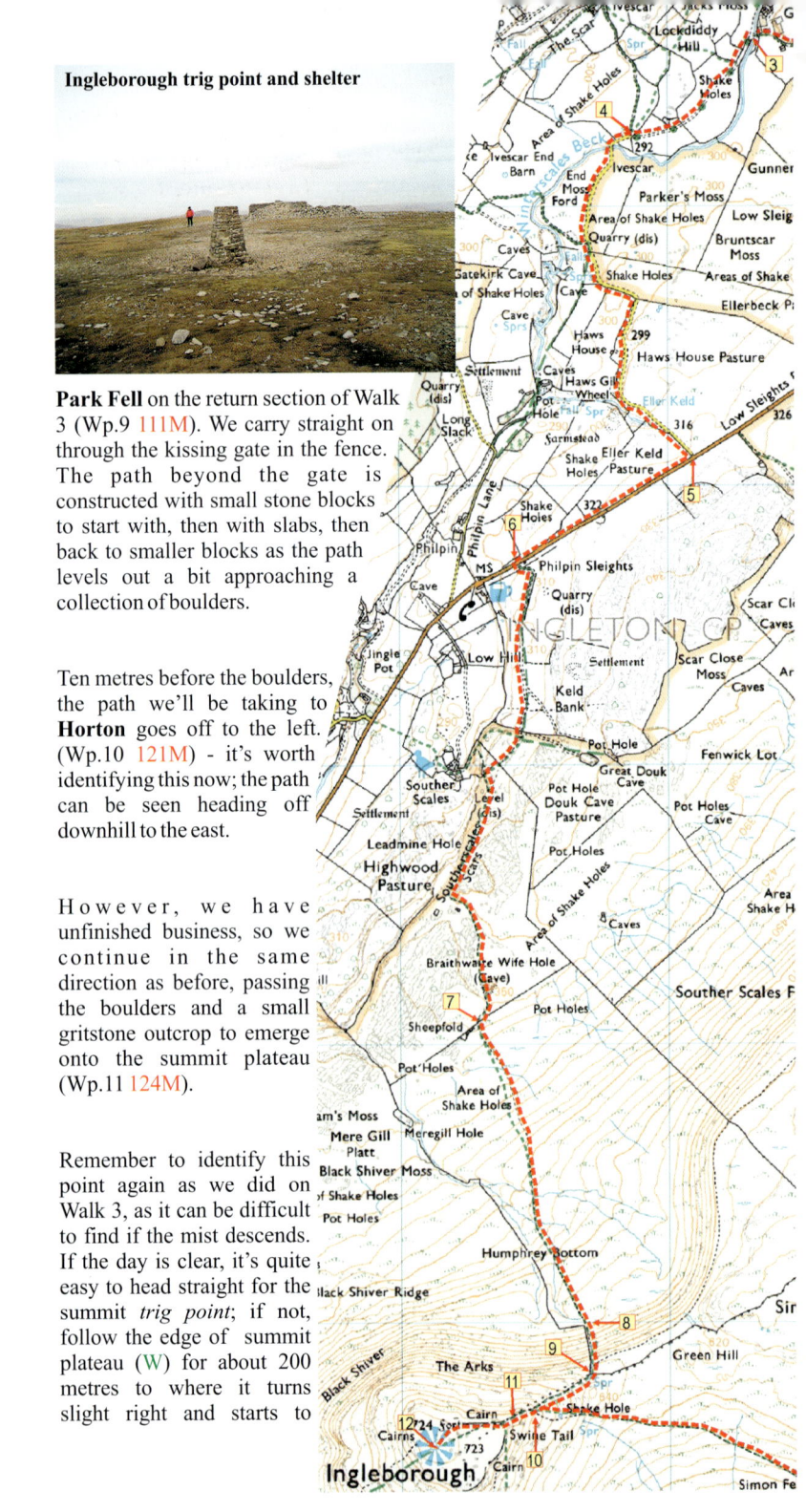

Park Fell on the return section of Walk 3 (Wp.9 111M). We carry straight on through the kissing gate in the fence. The path beyond the gate is constructed with small stone blocks to start with, then with slabs, then back to smaller blocks as the path levels out a bit approaching a collection of boulders.

Ten metres before the boulders, the path we'll be taking to **Horton** goes off to the left. (Wp.10 121M) - it's worth identifying this now; the path can be seen heading off downhill to the east.

However, we have unfinished business, so we continue in the same direction as before, passing the boulders and a small gritstone outcrop to emerge onto the summit plateau (Wp.11 124M).

Remember to identify this point again as we did on Walk 3, as it can be difficult to find if the mist descends. If the day is clear, it's quite easy to head straight for the summit *trig point*; if not, follow the edge of summit plateau (W) for about 200 metres to where it turns slight right and starts to descend. At this point we turn slight left and follow the worn stony section (SW) straight to the summit of **Ingleborough** (Wp.12 131M).

The summit has the *trig point*, the cross-shaped shelter, and as often as not a multitude of walkers, as this is a popular excursion from **Ingleton** and **Clapham**. Today is a training walk, so we have time to relax at the shelter or to explore the plateau. The next time we come this way will be on the Challenge walk, when there won't be time for either!

When finished at the top, reverse the last section of the ascent route through Wp.11 to the path junction to **Horton** (Wp.10 139M); it's here that we leave the ascent route and take the descending path to the right.

The start of the descent to Horton

Easy walking towards Horton

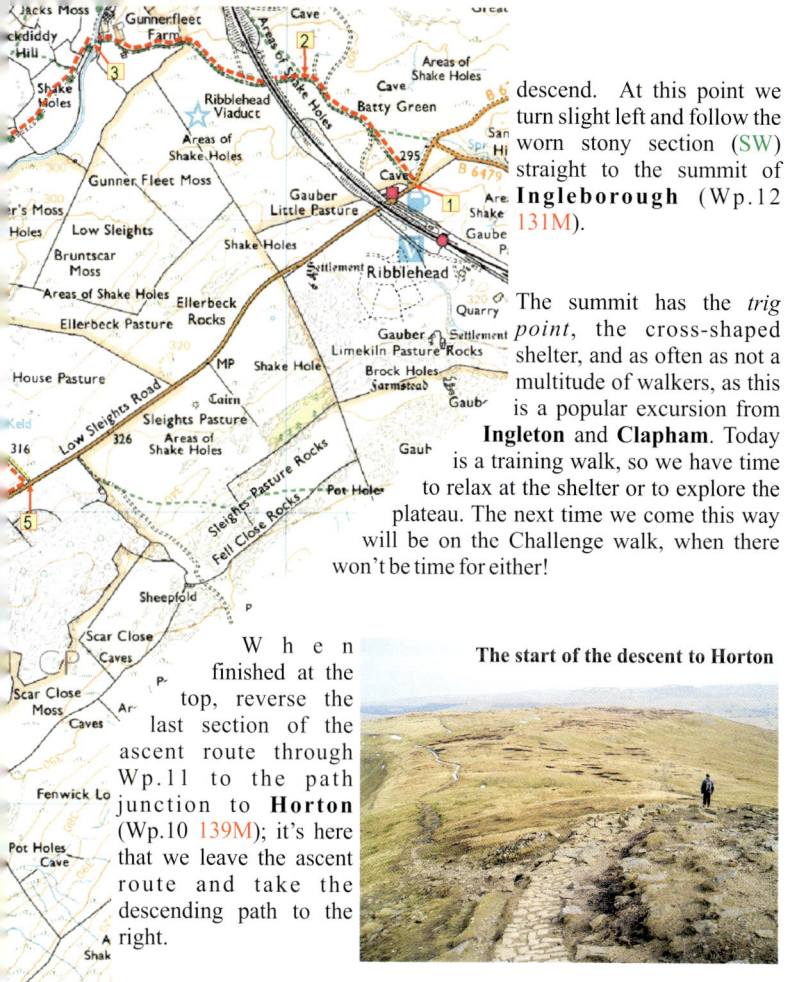

Paved at first, the path becomes steeper and is eroded, muddy and stony; before long, though, the path becomes less steep with flat(ish) easy walking to a ladder stile over a stone wall. Beyond there the path continues with easy walking towards an area of *limestone pavement* with **Pen y Ghent** visible in the distance, about 8 kms (5 miles) away.

A rougher section follows, with a short section of wooden boardwalk after that. We pass an old ruined stone shooting hut, and soon after that the path crosses a small beck, followed by a wooden gate, with a finger post indicating 'Horton 2¾ miles'.

Yorkshire 3 Peaks   **67**

The crossing of paths at Sulber (Wp.14)

Less than 100 metres on from the gate there is a Y-fork (Wp.13 183M), where we take the left fork following a wall on the left. The path moves towards the edge of a *limestone pavement*, and soon after goes through a wooden gate, then straight on in the same general direction.

The next feature is a crossing of paths at **Sulber** (Wp.14 200M). The fingerpost indicates 'Selside' to the left, 'Clapham' to the right, while we head straight on towards 'Horton', signed as 1½ miles away.

The section after the cross-paths is fairly featureless except for the path we're on. We continue to follow this through a wooden gate, where we now have our first glimpse of buildings at our journey's end in **Horton**.

About 200 metres beyond th gate we come to a fingerpost (Wp.15 219M) signing 'Austwick' to the right (3 ½ miles) and 'Horton' straight on (1 mile); there's also a small flattened cairn to right of the fingerpost. We carry on in the same direction as before, still heading towards **Horton**.

Not far beyond there, the path has been re-routed to the right by a low wooden rail. The faint original path can be seen heading straight on, while we continue on the new, more obvious path, following marker posts with yellow and green markings and the occasional cairn, bringing us to an information panel next to a wooden gate (Wp.16 230M).

The final section heading to Horton

Our path continues to a ladder stile with a small gate (Wp.17 236M) and 50 metres beyond the stile the farm track to **Beecroft Hall** crosses our way, but our path goes straight on, still easy to follow. About this time the **Horton Quarry** workings with a distinctive turquoise lagoon become visible.

We pass through a wooden gate, beyond which the path drops more steeply down to **Horton Railway Station**. A ramp takes us down to the railway line which we cross with care to the other platform; the gate directly ahead from the line crossing is the station exit and the road ahead descends towards **Horton** village. We carry straight on towards the **Crown Hotel**, then cross the wooden footbridge to finish at the car park (Wp.18 251M).

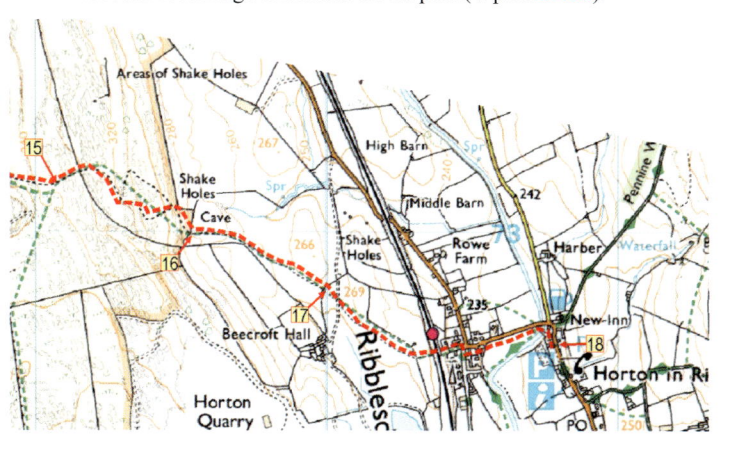

The **Crown**, **Golden Lion** or the **Pen y Ghent Café** are all near at hand so, preparation done, this is a good time to celebrate the completion of the

7 THE THREE PEAKS CHALLENGE

A long day out!

This is it - the big day. If you've completed the preceding walks you'll know the ground and that knowledge should give you confidence. You'll also be fitter than you were a few weeks back, which will give you that extra edge. So, guide in pocket, let's go and do the Three Peaks Challenge.

5+ | 11¾H | 21.75 miles 35km | 1570m / 1570m

! Refreshments? Forget it, you won't have time!

Access by car: This is a circular walk starting and finishing at **Horton in Ribblesdale** (for travel directions by car see Walk 1).

The route description is repeated here again in its entirety, to remove the necessity of flitting from one section of the guide to another. The way given on the second section (**Ribblehead** to the **Hill Inn**) is the one we took on Walk 5, though we have the option of taking the Walk 2 variation if this is preferred.

To make it easy to keep tabs on how long the walk is taking, the timings are given in hours and minutes (e.g. 1:30) rather than minutes (90M) as in the previous walks.

If 11 hours 51 minutes seems to be cutting it a bit fine for a 12 hour schedule, it's worth remembering that the research walks were done by the author between November and March, often in true winter conditions and on all but one of the walks, full winter clothing and equipment had to be carried. In addition, the pace of the walks was also dictated by the author's need to take photographs and to record notes. Without these distractions, and a lighter summer rucksack, most walkers will find the timings generous.

The first of the peaks - Pen y Ghent

THE FIRST PEAK; PEN Y GHENT

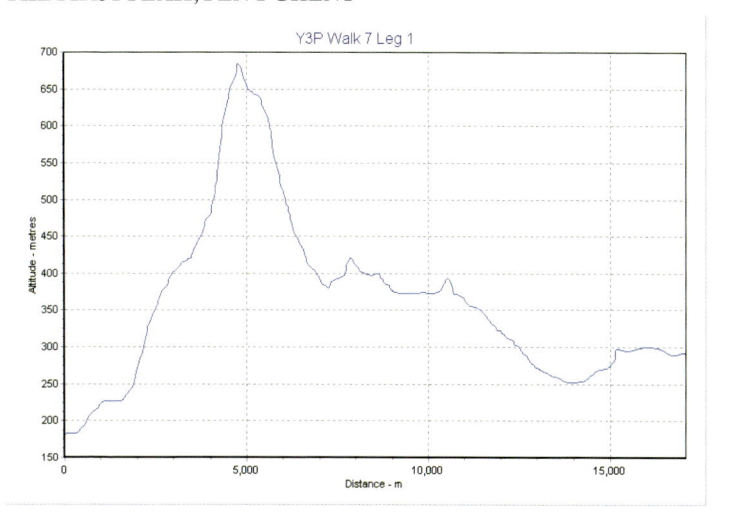

As this is the day of the Y3P Challenge, the start point is the **Pen y Ghent Café** (Wp.1 0:00) near the car park in **Horton**. As before we head towards **Settle**, passing the **Golden Lion**, and **St Oswald's Church**. After the church we take the second minor road on the left (Wp.2 0:08) following the lane with the beck on the left, passing the village school on the right. A little further on, the lane moves to the right away from the beck, heading towards **Brackenbottom** farmhouse (Wp.3 0:20). Here the route follows a footpath on the left, immediately before the first building, and signed to 'Pen y Ghent'.

After passing through a wooden gate, the path heads upwards (NE) with a stone wall running parallel on the left. The path crosses a wall by a step stile and continues gaining height (ENE) with the wall still on the left, passing through several small limestone outcrops and another step stile. Our route follows a short length of constructed path to a wooden gate in the wall (Wp.4 0:53). The path then continues gaining height including a section of causeway stones. After a short, steeper section another wall crosses our path and we come to a wooden gate (Wp.5 1:12), where we join the **Pennine Way**.

Here we turn left and continue upwards on a well-constructed path built from *gritstone* blocks. A little way above that, the path climbs a short limestone escarpment where there are several route options. The way continues upwards, passing through an area of boulders before climbing through another escarpment, this time *gritstone* instead of limestone.

The path then levels out to continue more easily to the summit (Wp.6 1:41) with its *trig point*, walled shelter and two small gate stiles that give access to the other side of the wall. Congratulations at this point on reaching the summit of **Pen y Ghent**, number one on our list.

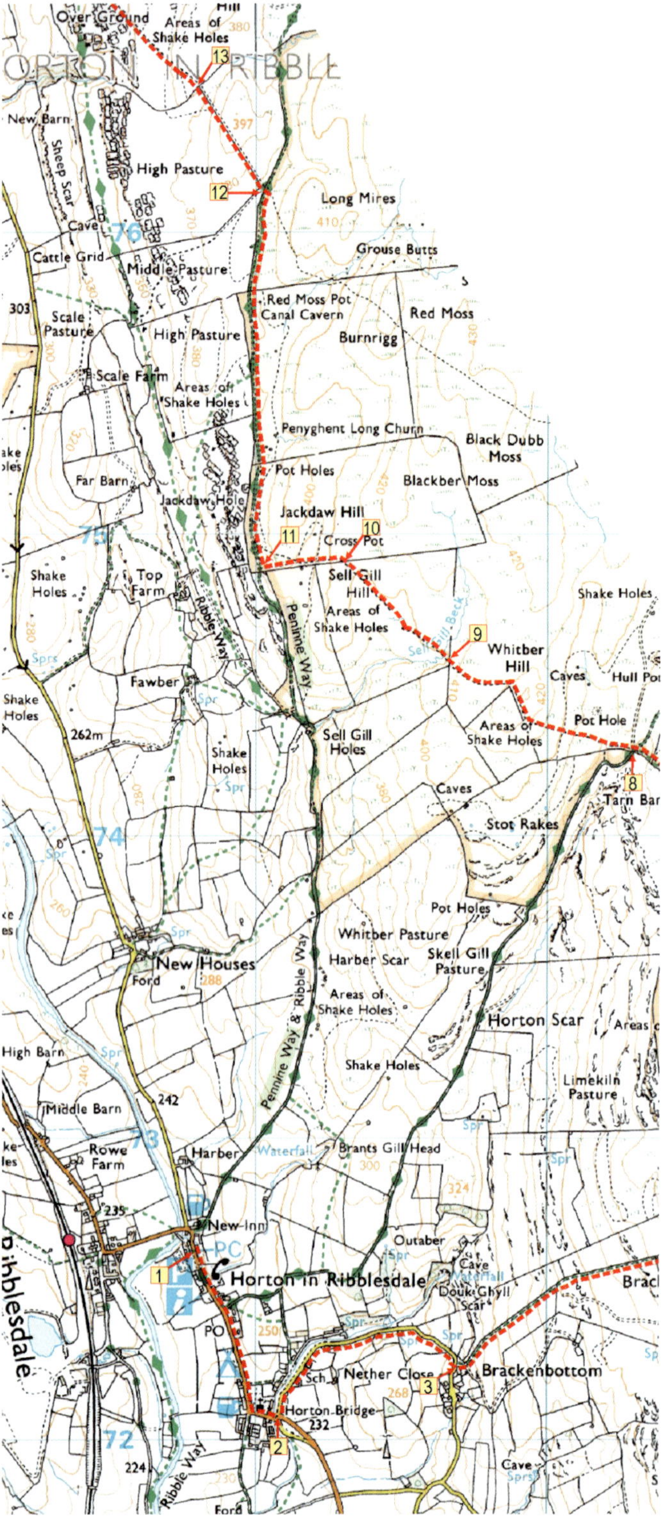

Over Ground
Hill
Areas of
Shake Holes
380
ORTON IN RIBBLE
13
397
New Barn
Sheep Scar
High Pasture
12
Long Mires
370
410
Cave
76
Grouse Butts
Cattle Grid
Middle Pasture
330
360
303
Red Moss Pot
Canal Cavern
Red Moss
Scale
Pasture
High Pasture
Burnrigg
430
300
380
Scale Farm
Areas of
Shake Holes
Penyghent Long Churn
320
Black Dubb
Moss
Pot Holes
Far Barn
Blackber Moss
400
420
Jackdaw Hole
Jackdaw Hill
75
11
10
Cross Pot
Shake
Holes
Top
Farm
Sell Gill
Hill
420
Shake Holes
Ribble Way
Areas of
Shake Holes
Pennine Way
280
9
Whitber
Hill
Sprs
Caves
Hull Pot
Fawber
Spr
410
420
Shake
Holes
Pot Hole
Areas of
Shake Holes
262m
Sell Gill
Holes
Shake
Holes
400
8
Spr
Tarn Bar
280
Caves
390
Stot Rakes
74
Spr
260
Pot Holes
Spr
Whitber Pasture
New Houses
Skell Gill
Pasture
Ford
Harber Scar
288
Ribble Way
Areas of
Shake Holes
Horton Scar
Areas o
High Barn
Spr
Shake Holes
Limekiln
Pasture
240
Pennine Way & Ribble Way
Middle Barn
242
Spr
Rowe
Farm
73
Harber
Waterfall
Brants Gill Head
300
Spr
324
235
New Inn
PC
Outaber
Ribblesdale
1
Horton in Ribblesdale
Cave
Waterfall
Douk Ghyll
Scar
Brac
PO
250
Spr
Spr
Spr
Sch
Nether Close
Brackenbottom
268
3
Horton Bridge
232
72
2
224
Ribble Way
230
Cave
Sprs
Ford

TO THE SECOND PEAK - WHERNSIDE

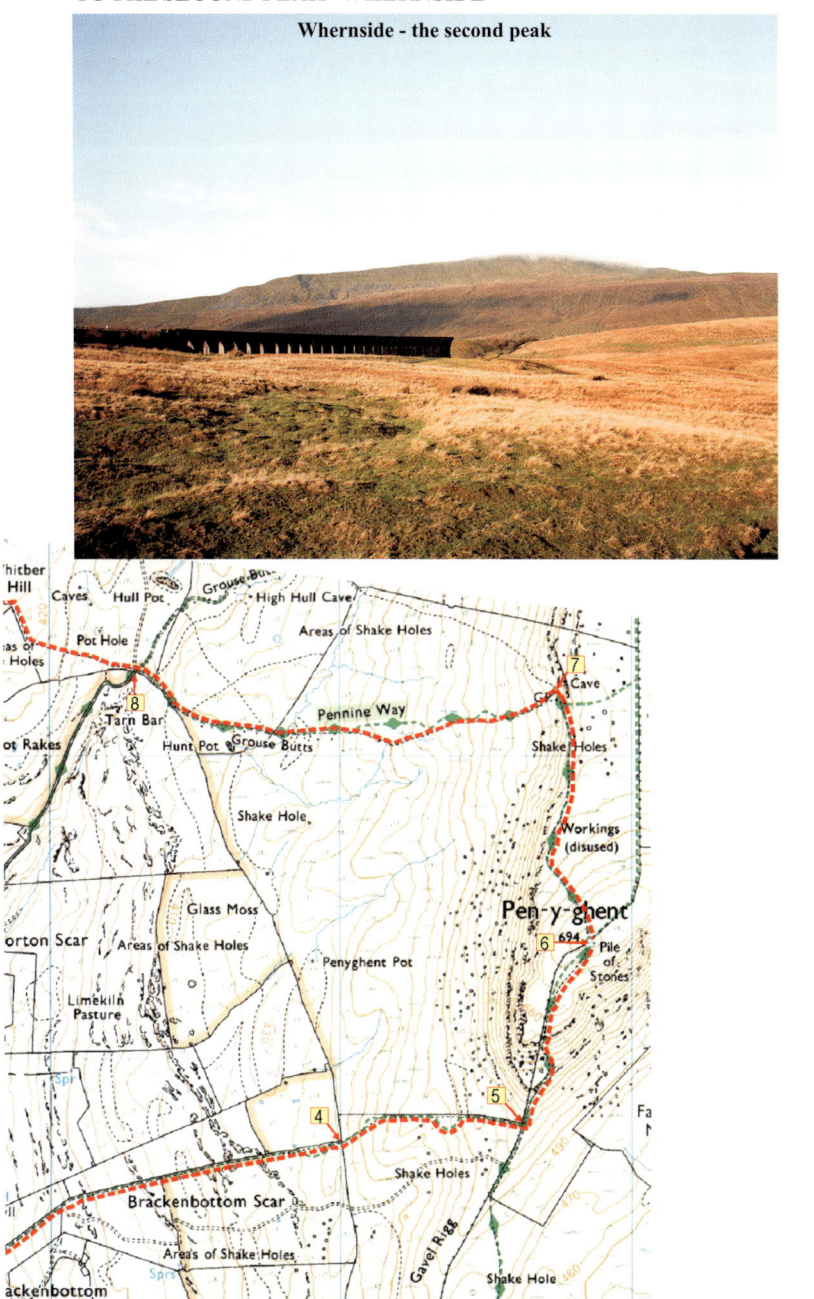

Whernside - the second peak

Yorkshire 3 Peaks 73

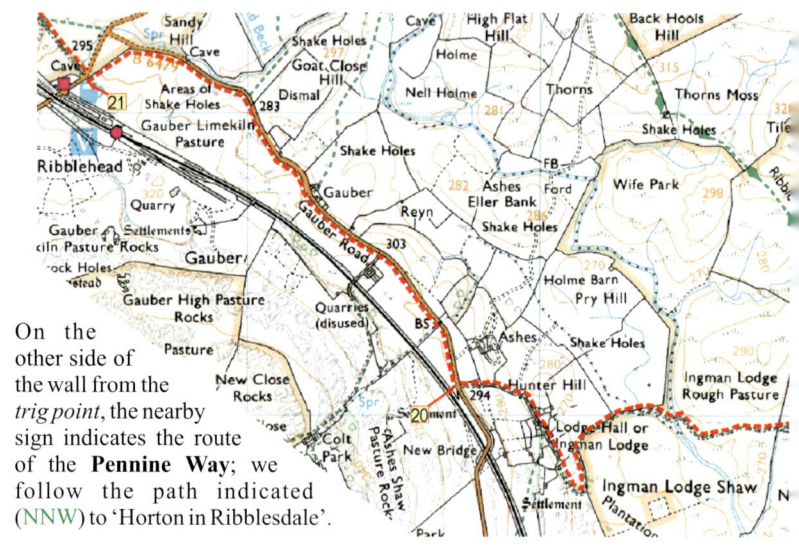

On the other side of the wall from the *trig point*, the nearby sign indicates the route of the **Pennine Way**; we follow the path indicated (NNW) to 'Horton in Ribblesdale'.

The scrappy path soon becomes more distinct as it descends, eventually turning more to the north, then running along the top of the steep western slopes of the mountain.

Our descent continues that way until it reaches a sharp left turn (Wp.7 2:13) next to a large, flattened cairn with a much fainter path going straight on. We take the left turn and continue down the good path in a mainly westerly direction.

As the downhill gradient begins to level out, we cross two walls using stiles to reach the junction with **Horton Lane** on the left and the detour to **Hull Pot** on the right (Wp.8 2:41).

Here we go straight on, following a fainter path that rises following the wall on the left for a little over 50 metres. The path and wall then start to diverge, but after 300 metres they come back together again. Here we turn right and walk with the wall on our left. In just over 100 metres the wall comes to a right angle corner to the left. The path appears to go straight on, but our path is the fainter one to the left, which gradually drifts away from the stone wall. After 200 metres this path descends gradually to a wooden gate next to a ramshackle stone wall (Wp.9 2:57).

We go through the gate, with one wall going diagonally left and the other one diagonally right. We follow a faint, sunken path that splits the angle of the two walls, crossing **Sell Gill Beck** almost immediately. The path becomes so faint that it disappears, but we continue in the same general direction (NW) over boggy ground towards a stone wall that runs across our line of travel. As the wall gets nearer, there is an obvious gate to head for (Wp.10 3:06).

We go through the gate and turn left to follow the wall downhill for almost 300 metres to a wide grassy track crossing our path (Wp.11 3:14); this is the **Pennine Way** and it goes through a gate in the wall we've been following on our left. We don't go left though; instead we turn right (N) and follow the **Pennine Way** for about twenty minutes with a stone wall on our left, passing through two stone walls along the way. About five minutes after passing

74 Yorkshire 3 Peaks

through the second wall we need to keep a lookout for a step stile on the left (Wp.12 3:36), which we use to cross the wall.

The next short section can be boggy. The path climbs slightly before descending gently to a slot stile in a wall (Wp.13 3:45). We go through the stile to follow the path (NW) which becomes fainter though still discernable, heading towards a section of *limestone pavement.* We keep this on our left, and join a farm track coming from our right (Wp.14 3:56).

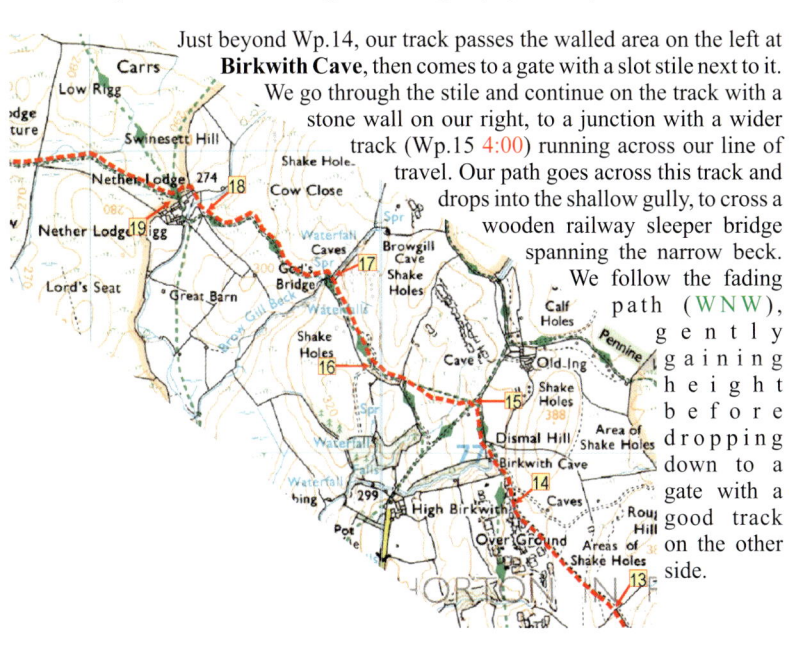

Just beyond Wp.14, our track passes the walled area on the left at **Birkwith Cave**, then comes to a gate with a slot stile next to it. We go through the stile and continue on the track with a stone wall on our right, to a junction with a wider track (Wp.15 4:00) running across our line of travel. Our path goes across this track and drops into the shallow gully, to cross a wooden railway sleeper bridge spanning the narrow beck. We follow the fading path (WNW), gently gaining height before dropping down to a gate with a good track on the other side.

We go through the gate and follow the track for about 100 metres, where it suddenly turns uphill to the right, next to a large limestone block and a wooden fingerpost (Wp.16 4:07). Here we go straight on next to the wall on

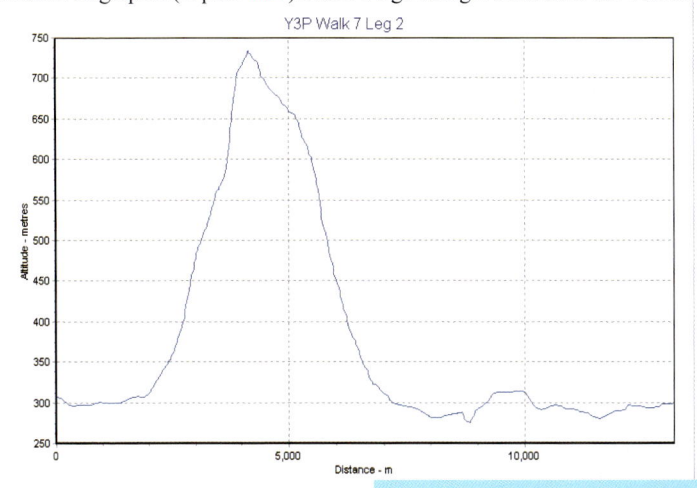

Yorkshire 3 Peaks 75

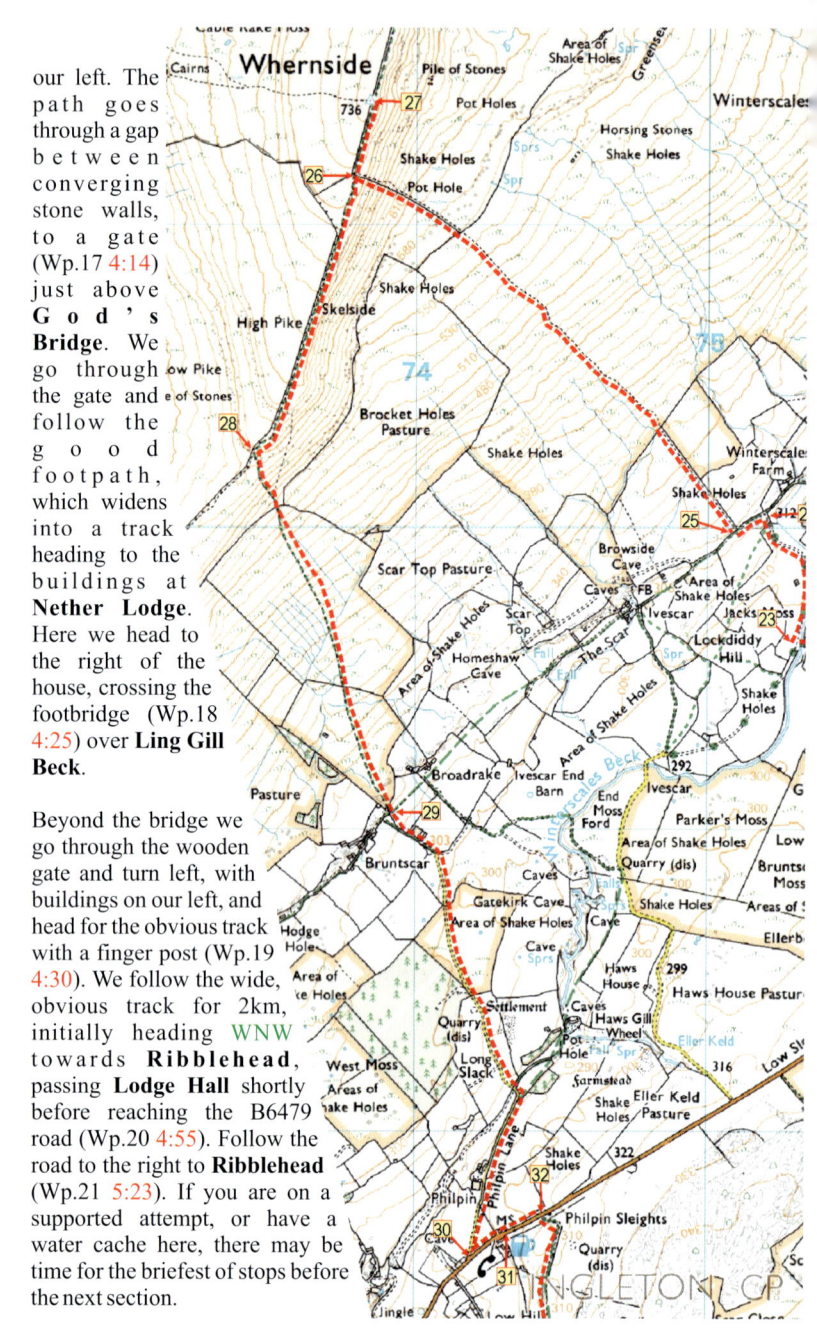

our left. The path goes through a gap between converging stone walls, to a gate (Wp.17 4:14) just above **God's Bridge**. We go through the gate and follow the good footpath, which widens into a track heading to the buildings at **Nether Lodge**. Here we head to the right of the house, crossing the footbridge (Wp.18 4:25) over **Ling Gill Beck**.

Beyond the bridge we go through the wooden gate and turn left, with buildings on our left, and head for the obvious track with a finger post (Wp.19 4:30). We follow the wide, obvious track for 2km, initially heading WNW towards **Ribblehead**, passing **Lodge Hall** shortly before reaching the B6479 road (Wp.20 4:55). Follow the road to the right to **Ribblehead** (Wp.21 5:23). If you are on a supported attempt, or have a water cache here, there may be time for the briefest of stops before the next section.

The start point for the next section is at the same place as for Walks 2 and 5, about 50 metres downhill from the **Station Inn** where a track leaves the roadside heading towards the railway viaduct (NW) with the railway line running parallel on the left. After 500 metres the path starts to curve left to head under the viaduct, with a line of boulders on the right hand side of the path (Wp.22 5:30). Unless following the Walk 2 variation, we follow the track as it bends to the left to pass under **Ribblehead Viaduct** and then continue to the bridge over **Winterscales Beck**, with **Gunnerfleet Farm** on our right. Just over the bridge, our track joins another track at a T-junction (Wp.23 5:38) where we turn right towards **Winterscales Farm**.

After passing through a gate, we arrive at another T-junction (Wp.24 5:45) and turn left, following the track (SW) for 100 metres to a ladder stile crossing the wall on our right (Wp.25 5:47). We cross the wall using the stile, then follow the grassy path heading upwards (NW) with a stone wall on the right. A second ladder stile follows and the path continues still climbing steeply in the same direction.

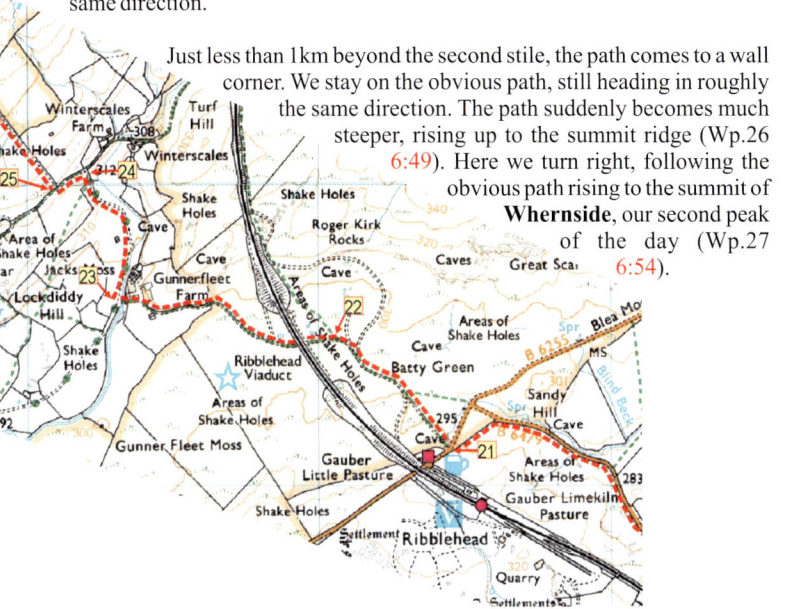

Just less than 1km beyond the second stile, the path comes to a wall corner. We stay on the obvious path, still heading in roughly the same direction. The path suddenly becomes much steeper, rising up to the summit ridge (Wp.26 6:49). Here we turn right, following the obvious path rising to the summit of **Whernside**, our second peak of the day (Wp.27 6:54).

ONWARD TO INGLEBOROUGH - THE THIRD PEAK

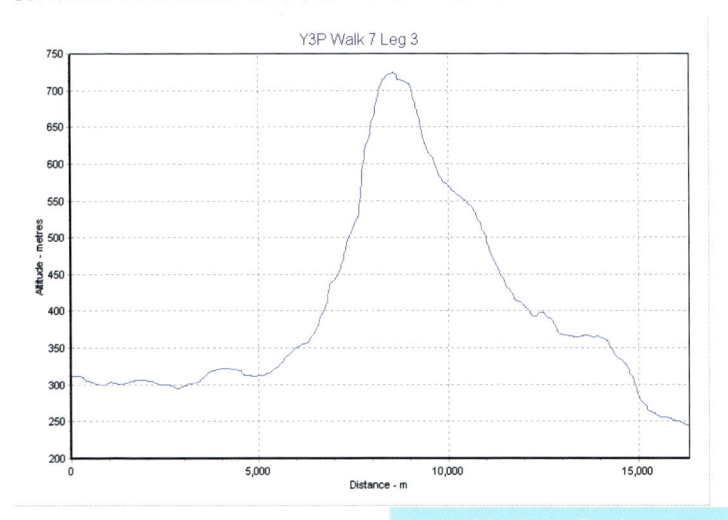

Yorkshire 3 Peaks 77

Time is pressing, so after the briefest of celebrations we reverse the last section of ridge, going back to Wp.26. Now we ignore the steep path we came up on and pass through the gate in front of us. Our path continues descending (SSW) for about 1km to where the well-defined path suddenly turns to the left heading downhill, and a faint path carries straight on, descending next to the wall (Wp.28 7:18); we take the well-defined path descending to the left.

After a steep section we cross two stone walls, the first by step stiles, the second by ladder stiles, until the path goes through a gate with a small stone barn on the left. Just beyond the barn, the path comes to a T-junction with a bridleway (Wp.29 8:04).

On the bridleway we turn right, and in 30 metres come to a junction to the left, with the blue road sign with a white arrow. From here we go left and follow the track, then tarmac lane, descending gently in a southerly direction for about 1km. The lane turns to the right and climbs a little to **Philpin Farm**. From there we carry on down the lane to meet the **Ingleton** to **Hawes** road (Wp.30 8:23).

We turn left and walk up the road for a little over 100 metres to the **Hill Inn** (Wp.31 8:26) but no time to stop today. Instead we walk up the road (NE) for almost 200 metres to the gate on the right (Wp.32 8:28) with the small water-works building just beyond. This is a good place to meet up with support or to collect cached water. Again, the stop needs to be brief, as the final section over **Ingleborough** beckons.

It's time for the last obstacle as **Ingleborough** looms ahead. As before, we follow the good track signed for 'Great Douk and Ingleborough', passing through three gates in succession, the third gate being the entrance to **Southerscales Nature Reserve**. Just past the huge *shakehole* of **Braithwaite Wife Hole** on our left, we reach a pair of step stiles with gates (Wp.33 8:59), with a causeway path beyond on the other side of the wall.

78 Yorkshire 3 Peaks

Ingleborough, the third peak, looms ahead

The causeway path climbs steadily, eventually levelling out in a dip just below where the path suddenly steepens (Wp.34 9:22). A set of well-constructed steps climb the steep bit and as this section levels out, we cross the stream where the path goes left to **Park Fell** on the return section of Walk 3 (Wp.35 9:31). We carry straight on to a kissing gate in the fence. The path is constructed with small stone blocks to start with, then slabs, then back to smaller blocks as the path levels out a bit approaching a collection of boulders. Ten metres before the boulders, the path to **Horton** goes off to the left. (Wp.36 9:41). It's worth identifying this now; the path we will take to **Horton** can be seen heading off downhill to the east.

We continue in the same direction as before, passing the boulders and a small gritstone outcrop to emerge onto the summit plateau (Wp.37 9:44). Remember to identify this point, as it can be difficult to find if the mist descends. If the day is clear, it's quite easy to head straight for the summit *trig point*; if not, follow the edge of summit plateau (W) for about 200 metres to

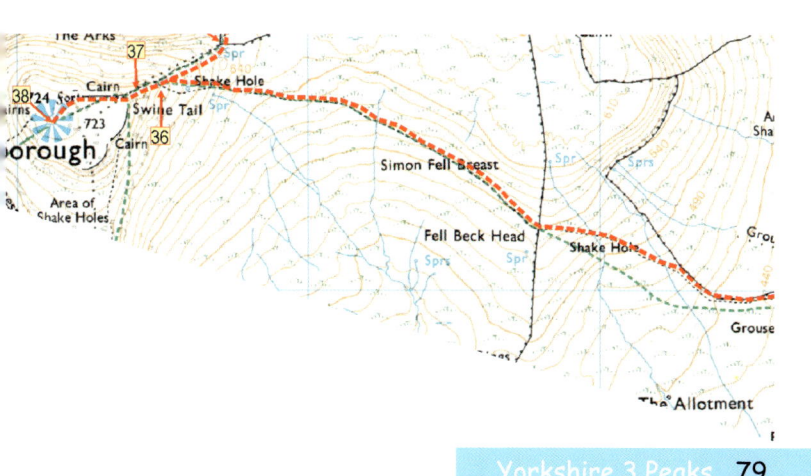

Yorkshire 3 Peaks 79

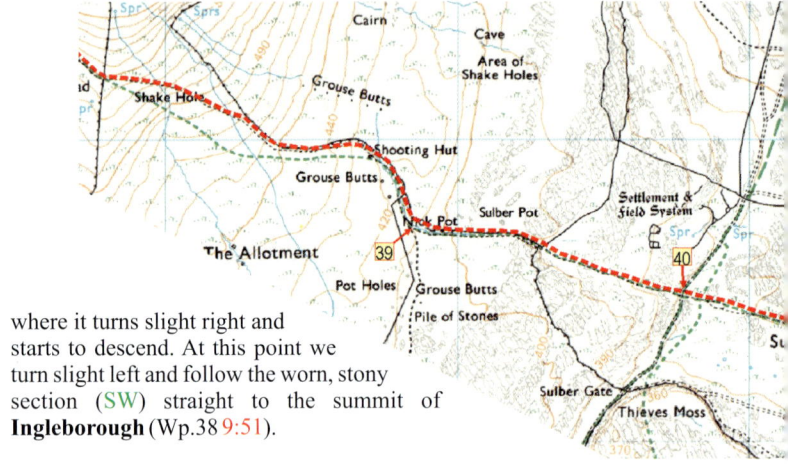

where it turns slight right and
starts to descend. At this point we
turn slight left and follow the worn, stony
section (SW) straight to the summit of
Ingleborough (Wp.38 9:51).

This summit should be familiar ground now: as the last of the
Three Peaks, it comes as a welcome sight. There's little time available for
celebrations just now, though, as we still have to get back to **Horton**. So, when
finished at the top, reverse the last section of the ascent route through Wp.37,
back to the path junction to **Horton** (Wp.36 9:59).

The path is paved at first, but it then becomes steeper, and is eroded, muddy
and stony. Before long the path becomes less steep, with flat(ish) easy
walking to a ladder stile over a stone wall. Beyond there the path continues
with easy walking towards an area of *limestone pavement*, with **Pen y Ghent**
visible in the distance, about 8kms (5 miles) away.

A rougher path follows, with a short section of wooden boardwalk after that.
We pass an old, ruined stone shooting hut, and soon after that the path crosses
a small beck, followed by a wooden gate, with a finger post indicating 'Horton
2 ¾ miles'. Less than 100 metres on from the gate there's a Y-fork (Wp.39
10:43) where we take the left fork, following a wall on the left.

The path moves towards the edge of a *limestone pavement*, and soon after
goes through a wooden gate, then straight on in the same general direction.

The next feature is a crossing of paths at **Sulber** (Wp.40 11:00). The
fingerpost indicates 'Selside' to the left, 'Clapham' to the right, and 'Horton'
straight on, 1½ miles away; we go straight on.

The section after the cross-paths is fairly featureless except for the path we're
on. We continue to follow this through a wooden gate, where we now have our
first glimpse of buildings at our journey's end in **Horton**. About 200 metres
beyond the gate we come to a fingerpost (Wp.41 11.19), signing 'Austwick' to
the right (3½ miles) and 'Horton' straight on (1 mile). There is also a small,
flattened cairn to the right of the fingerpost. We carry on in the same direction
as before, still heading towards **Horton**.

Not far beyond there the path has been re-routed to the right by a low wooden
rail; the faint original path can be seen heading straight on, but we continue on
the new, more obvious path, following marker posts with yellow and green

80 Yorkshire 3 Peaks

markings and the occasional cairn, bringing us to an information panel next to a wooden gate (Wp.42 11:30).

Our path continues to a ladder stile with a small gate (Wp.43 11:36) and 50 metres beyond the stile, the farm track to **Beecroft Hall** crosses our way, but our path goes straight on, still easy to follow, with **Horton Quarry** coming into view.

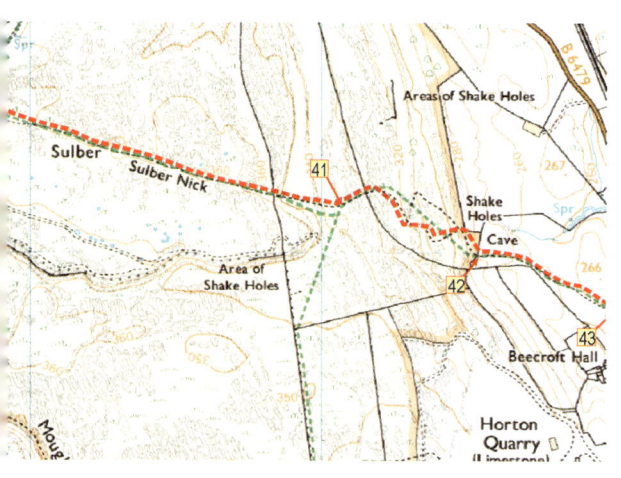

We pass through a wooden gate, beyond which the path drops more steeply down to **Horton Railway Station**. A ramp takes us down to the railway line, which we cross with care to the other platform. The gate directly ahead from the line crossing is the station exit and the road ahead descends towards **Horton** village. We carry straight on towards the **Crown Hotel**, then cross the wooden footbridge, passing the car park to finish at the **Pen y Ghent Café** (Wp.44 11:51).

With our Three Peak Challenge completed, it's good to ponder on the 35km (22 miles) distance and 1570 metres (5150 feet) ascent covered on the route. Add to that the training and preparation, and there are plenty of reasons for congratulations and celebrations. You probably don't need a guide to help with that!

Yorkshire 3 Peaks 81

AFTER THE THREE PEAKS CHALLENGE

Now what?

For some, the Yorkshire Three Peaks Challenge will be a once in a lifetime experience. In fact, some will be glad if they never set foot on a hill again. Ever! Others, though, will be inspired to go on and enjoy bigger mountain challenges. But where to start? What to do? Here are a few ideas that might serve as pointers to continuing a lifetime of challenges.

Those who have completed all the walks in this book should have a fairly good knowledge of this area by now, so one possibility is to go for new challenges in the Yorkshire Three Peaks area. So, how about the following for ideas?

Pen y Ghent at sunset

- Do the Challenge route, but do it faster – Learn how to cut down on the weight carried, and build up running fitness. My best time is a little under six hours, but the real runners do it in less than three hours.

Winter walkers head for Pen y Ghent.

- Do some of the walks, and eventually the Challenge route, at night. Navigation needs to be absolutely spot on, but the Three Peaks are something completely different in the dark.

The final section to Pen y Ghent summit

- Try some of the walks in winter conditions. A different sort of challenge altogether. Remember, though, that the days are much shorter, and that these hills can be unbelievably wild in winter. A blizzard here is not unknown, and could be life threatening.

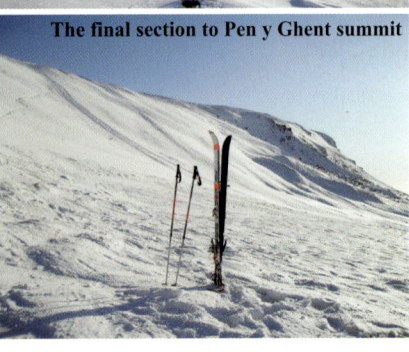

- Having looked at some Yorkshire Dales possibilities, there are also worthy options to consider in other mountain areas. Let's start with the Lake District.

- Cumbria was once three counties. A circuit of the three highest "Old County Tops" of **Scafell Pike** (Cumberland), **Helvellyn** (Westmoreland) and **Coniston Old Man** (Lancashire) takes about sixteen hours.

- The lakes "Three Thousands" circuit - Three Lake District peaks over 3000 ft high (**Skiddaw**, **Scafell Pike** and **Helvellyn**) all in one go. About twenty-four hours needed for this.

- For the elite or masochistic, the **Bob Graham Round** is worth considering. A circuit of 42 peaks to be completed in twenty four hours - 72 miles and almost the height of Everest from sea level. First completed in 1932 by Bob Graham, and not repeated until 1960. For further details see *http://www.bobgrahamclub.co.uk*

In North Wales another challenge route awaits - **The Welsh Three Thousands Challenge**.

This involves visiting the tops of all fifteen of the mountains over 3000 ft in Wales within the space of twenty-four hours. The length is about twenty-four miles, but you have to walk up to the start point and down from the finish point, which can take it to over thirty miles in total. Although twenty-four hours is the accepted time, many aim to do it in twelve. It has been run in a little over four hours!

For those who prefer distance to speed, there is the famous **Pennine Way** walk or the **West Highland Way** in Scotland. **Wainwright's Coast-to-Coast** walk and a host of **Scottish Coast-to-Coast** routes add more possibilities.

Snowdon - the highest peak in Wales

And there is, of course, the National Three Peaks Challenge of **Snowdon**, **Scafell Pike** and **Ben Nevis**. If that sounds interesting, Discovery Walking Guides' '**The National 3 Peaks - Taking Up The Challenge**' by Steve Williams, is recommended reading.

SOME FINAL THOUGHTS

Some final thoughts.

The Yorkshire Three Peaks Challenge, although popular, doesn't seem to excite the imagination as much as the National Three Peaks Challenge. This is a pity, because the Yorkshire Challenge has a lot going for it. The National Challenge may have higher hills, but size isn't everything, and the smaller hills of the Yorkshire Three Peaks have a sense of integrity, with all the peaks being visited in one walk.

Damage caused by boots and water

However, challenge walks can have an adverse impact on the terrain, on communities and the environment, but the Yorkshire Challenge is, in some ways, less damaging than the National. Routes followed by large numbers of people are eventually going to become worn and eroded, and the Yorkshire Challenge is no different in this regard, but the area is looked after and maintained by one body, the Yorkshire Dales National Park Authority.

An eroded path near Ingelborough

On the other hand, the National Challenge uses paths maintained by two different national parks (Snowdonia and the Lake District) and a charity (The Nevis Partnership). This means that if you wish to contribute financially to the maintenance of paths, it is much easier to make one single donation to the Yorkshire Dales National Park Authority than to three different bodies in three different countries. In fact, some of the major charities organising sponsored hill-walking events already contribute to path maintenance on the Y3P route.

Footpath maintenance itself is a controversial subject. Any footpath construction project is going to remove the wilderness factor from the hills, but the alternatives are equally undesirable. It is sometimes a choice between a stone causeway, visible from miles away, or an ever widening morass, where walkers try to avoid the boggy bits by walking round the sides. Before footpath construction started, the path to **Ingleborough** from **The Hill Inn** used to expand to a width of twenty or so metres. The current stone causeway is blending in with the surrounding countryside, and isn't the eyesore that the old path used to be. What's more, your feet stay dry.

An established causeway path blending in well

The area of the Three Peaks is no longer a wilderness, nor will it ever be again, but concentrating conservation efforts on 'honey pot' areas such as the Three Peaks is more effective, and reduces pressure on other areas. Trying to devise a cohesive maintenance strategy for Snowdonia, the Lakes and Ben Nevis altogether must be nigh on impossible.

The impact on communities can also be a problem. Participants in the National Challenge may well put money into the local economies of Llanberis and Fort William, but Wasdale Head gets nothing out of the deal, except traffic jams. The road infrastructure of the Lake District can become overwhelmed by the sheer number of vehicles supporting challenge participants, but local businesses rarely benefit. The Yorkshire Challenge, on the other hand, doesn't rely on participants being ferried around by vehicle, and local businesses do reap the benefit of an influx of visitors who spend money on food, accommodation and celebratory pints in the pubs.

The National Challenge also has a much larger carbon footprint than the Yorkshire Challenge. It is almost a 500 mile drive to link the three national summits, and that's not including travel to and from the start and finish points. It has often been said that the National Challenge is as much a test of the commitment and determination of the drivers as that of the walkers, but one journey will get you to **Horton in Ribblesdale**, with no need then to drive long distances to support walkers.

Well-maintained repairs - Ingleborough

The National Three Peaks Challenge is destined to remain popular, as it includes the highest mountains of England, Scotland and Wales, and for many this would be the challenge and aspiration of a lifetime. The Yorkshire Three Peaks Challenge, on the other hand, causes less impact on the land, the local community and the environment, and is easier to keep maintained.

On top of that it is an individual and worthwhile physical challenge that doesn't depend on direct support, yet is achievable by many.

So, what are you waiting for?

GPS WAYPOINTS & CO-ORDINATES

For advice on using GPS as a navigational aid see pages 34 & 35 of this book.

INPUTTING GPS WAYPOINTS FOR THE YORKSHIRE THREE PEAKS

GPS Waypoints are quoted for the OSGB datum and BNG position format. To input the Waypoints into your GPS we suggest that you:-

- switch on your GPS and select 'simulator', 'demo' or 'operate with GPS off' mode,

- check that your GPS is set to the OSGB datum and the BNG position format; see your GPS manual for instructions,

- input the GPS Waypoints into a 'GPS route' with the same number as the walking route number; then there should be no confusion as to which walking route it refers,

- repeat the inputting of routes until you have covered all your planned walking routes,

- turn off your GPS. When you turn the GPS back on it should return to its normal navigation mode.

Note that GPS Waypoints complement the detailed walking route descriptions, and are not intended for use as an alternative to the route description.

1 PEN Y GHENT from HORTON

Wp	Zn	Easting	Northing
1	SD	80779	72597
2	SD	81084	72077
3	SD	81688	72273
4	SD	82998	72732
5	SD	83618	72788
6	SD	83850	73389
7	SD	83739	74223
8	SD	82301	74284
9	SD	81090	72505
10	SD	80894	72439
11	SD	80776	72610

2 WHERNSIDE from RIBBLEHEAD

Wp	Zn	Easting	Northing
1	SD	76510	79099
2	SD	76094	79479
3	SD	76093	81648
4	SD	75711	82447
5	SD	73861	81433
6	SD	73808	81169
7	SD	73446	80238
8	SD	73914	79058
9	SD	74729	79735
10	SD	75088	79995
11	SD	75176	80061
12	SD	75315	79624
13	SD	76069	79496
14	SD	76441	79129

3 INGLEBOROUGH from THE HILL INN

Wp	Zn	Easting	Northing
1	SD	74452	77724
2	SD	74447	77119
3	SD	74298	76243
4	SD	74290	76092
5	SD	74666	75015
6	SD	74712	74843
7	SD	74697	74819
8	SD	74481	74699
9	SD	74408	74669
10	SD	74229	74654
11	SD	74124	74570
12	SD	74127	74605
13	SD	74713	74837
14	SD	75215	75720
15	SD	75824	76420
16	SD	76519	77101
17	SD	76807	77625
18	SD	77169	77898
19	SD	76088	78070
20	SD	75703	77766
21	SD	75324	77500
22	SD	74959	77079
23	SD	74771	77045
24	SD	74451	77127
25	SD	74452	77724

4
HORTON to RIBBLEHEAD via PEN Y GHENT

Wp	Zn	Easting	Northing
1	SD	80779	72597
2	SD	81084	72077
3	SD	81688	72273
4	SD	82998	72732
5	SD	83618	72788
6	SD	83850	73389
7	SD	83739	74223
8	SD	82301	74284
9	SD	81664	74565
10	SD	81296	74902
11	SD	81009	74878
12	SD	81029	76149
13	SD	80798	76478
14	SD	80455	76863
15	SD	80310	77171
16	SD	79974	77283
17	SD	79827	77582
18	SD	79390	77822
19	SD	79273	77858
20	SD	77738	78090
21	SD	76453	79130

5
RIBBLEHEAD, WHERNSIDE, THE HILL INN, RIBBLEHEAD

Wp	Zn	Easting	Northing
1	SD	76435	79139
2	SD	76094	79479
3	SD	75319	79621
4	SD	75196	80042
5	SD	75102	79997
6	SD	73808	81169
7	SD	73853	81416
8	SD	73446	80238
9	SD	73913	79047
10	SD	74196	77588
11	SD	74300	77654
12	SD	74460	77738
13	SD	75089	78109
14	SD	74856	79252
15	SD	75308	79611
16	SD	76443	79131

6
RIBBLEHEAD, THE HILL INN, INGLEBOROUGH, HORTON

Wp	Zn	Easting	Northing
1	SD	76435	79127
2	SD	76084	79484
3	SD	75316	79620
4	SD	74858	79252
5	SD	75096	78111
6	SD	74444	77730
7	SD	74291	76093
8	SD	74664	75025
9	SD	74712	74854
10	SD	74485	74704
11	SD	74412	74669
12	SD	74133	74556
13	SD	76850	73710
14	SD	77759	73503
15	SD	79047	73177
16	SD	79534	73001
17	SD	79990	72812
18	SD	79990	72812

7
THE THREE PEAKS CHALLENGE

Wp	Zn	Easting	Northing
1	SD	80774	72613
2	SD	81084	72077
3	SD	81688	72273
4	SD	82998	72732
5	SD	83618	72788
6	SD	83850	73389
7	SD	83739	74223
8	SD	82301	74284
9	SD	81664	74565
10	SD	81296	74902
11	SD	81009	74878
12	SD	81029	76149
13	SD	80798	76478
14	SD	80455	76863
15	SD	80310	77171
16	SD	79974	77283
17	SD	79827	77582
18	SD	79390	77822
19	SD	79273	77858
20	SD	77738	78090
21	SD	76453	79130
22	SD	76094	79479
23	SD	75319	79621
24	SD	75196	80042
25	SD	75102	79997
26	SD	73808	81169
27	SD	73853	81416
28	SD	73446	80238
29	SD	73913	79047
30	SD	74196	77588
31	SD	74300	77654
32	SD	74460	77738
33	SD	74291	76093
34	SD	74664	75025
35	SD	74712	74854
36	SD	74485	74704
37	SD	74412	74669
38	SD	74133	74556
39	SD	76850	73710
40	SD	77759	73503
41	SD	79047	73177
42	SD	79534	73001
43	SD	79990	72812
44	SD	80774	72613

ACCOMMODATION

Horton in Ribblesdale has the greatest choice for accommodation, pubs and food, and there are also alternatives at **Ribblehead** and **Chapel le Dale**. The start points for the walks in the book are shown below, but by using a car or the train any of the locations could be used as a base

Horton in Ribblesdale
Walks 1, 4, 7 (The Challenge route)
The Crown Hotel BD24 0HF
Tel: 01729 860209
www.crown-hotel.co.uk
Real ale, food, B&B accommodation (also self catering cottages)

The Crown, Horton

The Golden Lion, Horton

The Golden Lion Hotel BD24 0HB
Tel: 01729 860206
www.goldenlionhotel.co.uk
Real ale, food, B&B accommodation (also camping)

3 Peaks Bunkroom BD24 0HB
Tel: 01729 860380
www.3peaksbunkroom.co.uk
Bunkhouse accommodation

Blindbeck BD24 0HT
Tel: 01729 860396
www.blindbeck.co.uk
Self-catering cottage

The Knoll BD24 0HD
Tel: 01729 860283
www.thepennineway.co.uk/theknoll
B&B accommodation

Holme Farm BD24 0HD
Tel: 01729 860281
Camping

Cragg Hill Farm BD24 0HW
Tel: 01729 860266
Camping

Pen y Ghent Café, Horton

Pen y Ghent Café BD24 0HE
Tel: 01729 860333
Food, traditional start point for the Three Peaks Challenge with booking in and out facility (see "Other useful information")

There is also a useful village shop in **Horton** for your grocery needs.

Ribblehead
Walks 2, 5, 6

The Station Inn LA6 3AS
Tel: 01524 241274
www.thestationinn.net
Real ale, food, B&B and bunkhouse accommodation.

The Station Inn, Ribblehead

Chapel le Dale
Walk 3

The Hill Inn, Chapel le Dale

Hill Inn LA6 3AR
Tel: 01524 241256
www.oldhillinn.co.uk
Real ale, food, B&B accommodation, Caravan Club site (5 units)

The Old School Bunkhouse
LA6 3AR
Tel: 01729 823835
www.oldschoolbunkhouse.co.uk
Bunkhouse accommodation

There are also alternatives at **Settle** or **Ingleton**

OTHER USEFUL INFORMATION

TOURIST INFORMATION

Pen-y-Ghent Café, Horton-in-Ribblesdale, BD24 0HE, Tel: 01729 860333

This is also the traditional start point for the Challenge Walk, with an antique clock card machine that will record your start and finish times for the walk (See below for more details)

The Community Centre, Ingleton, LA6 3HG, Tel: 01524 241049

The Town Hall, Settle, BD24 9EJ, Tel: 01729 825192

NHS CLINICS & DOCTORS, HOSPITALS & MEDICAL SERVICES

Townhead Surgery, Settle, BD24 9HZ, Tel: 01729 822205

Ingleton Surgery, High Street, Ingleton, LA6 3AB, Tel: 015242 61202 or 41732

Airedale General Hospital, Steeton, Keighley, BD20 6TD, Tel: 01535 652511

Royal Lancaster Infirmary, Ashton Road, Lancaster, LA1 4RP, Tel: 01524 65944

Bank View Pharmacy, Main Street, Ingleton, LA6 3EH, Tel: 01524 241154

Alliance Pharmacy, Market Place, Settle, BD24 9ED, Tel: 01729 822539

POLICE

In emergency dial 999 or 112

Settle Police Station (open Tuesdays 9-5pm & Saturdays 9-1pm) Duke Street, Settle, BD24 9DU, Tel: 0845 6060 247

Ingleton Police Station (open Fridays 9-5pm) Backgate, Ingleton LA6 3BT, Tel: 0845 6060 247

MOUNTAIN RESCUE

Dial 999 or 112, ask for North Yorkshire Police, and when connected ask for Mountain Rescue

GARAGES/PETROL STATIONS (Petrol & Diesel)

Church Street, Settle (on the B6480) BD24 9JD

New Road, Ingleton (on the A65) LA6 3DL

OUTDOOR EQUIPMENT & CLOTHING SHOPS

Cave & Crag, Market Place, Settle, BD24 9ED

Castleberg Outdoors, Cheapside, Settle, BD24 9EW

Daleswear, New Road, Ingleton, LA6 3HL

Inglesport, The Square, Ingleton, LA6 3EB

Bernie's Café, 4 Main Street, Ingleton, Via Carnforth, LA6 3EB

PEN Y GHENT CAFÉ BOOKING OUT-AND-IN SERVICE

This free service records your start and finish times for the Challenge Walk and is an excellent safety control - if you do not book in on your return they will take steps to ensure that you have returned safely. It's also the home of the Three Peaks Club.

Ask for your clock card, and write your name, home address, telephone number, vehicle registration and where the vehicle is parked. You then stamp the card in the clock machine and hand it back to the café. When you have completed the Yorkshire Three Peaks Challenge Walk, inform the café that you have returned and their staff will stamp your card. If you have completed the walk within 12 hours, you'll be invited to join the Three Peaks of Yorkshire Club, which entitles you to wear the Three Peaks Club badge.

Opening hours are 9-6pm weekdays (except Tuesday) and 8-6pm on Saturdays and Sundays. (The clock card service operates every day except Tuesdays and Fridays).

Walkers starting before the café opens can post their details through the door and the staff will create and stamp a card for you if you provide your name, home address, telephone number (home, work, or mobile), vehicle registration number, where the vehicle is parked and your start time (no cheating!).

GLOSSARY

GEOLOGY

cave	an underground passage, usually horizontal, formed by water action
clints	the flat, block-like surface of a limestone pavement, with the blocks separated by grikes
grikes	a crevice formed in limestone pavements by water erosion, separating the clints
gritstone	a coarse form of sandstone, prevalent in the north of England, formerly used to make millstones
limestone pavement	flat horizontal slabs of limestone, eroded by water into clints and grikes
pothole	an underground passage, usually vertical, formed by water action
shakehole	a steep depression caused by the ground collapsing into a sinkhole, sometimes with a stream sink or cave entrance
sinkhole/swallow hole	a hole formed by water action, taking surface drainage to a cave or pothole
resurgence	a spring or stream emerging to the surface from underground

NORTHERN NAMES FOR PHYSICAL FEATURES DERIVED FROM OLD NORSE WORDS

(Original Old Norse in brackets)

beck (bekkr)	stream
dale (dalur)	valley
fell (fjall)	hill
force or foss (fors)	waterfall
gill (gjel)	ravine or gorge
scales (skali)	summer pasture
scar (skera)	crag
tarn (tjarn)	small lake
thwaite (tveit)	clearing

HILLCRAFT & NAVIGATION

base layer	a thin layer of clothing worn next to the skin, transmitting moisture away from the body by a process known as 'wicking'
collecting feature	an obvious physical feature on the ground and map, such as a stream or road, which indicates that the objective has been over-shot
exposure	a medical condition also known as hypothermia, where the body becomes chilled to the extent that the core temperature of the trunk drops, causing a deterioration in body functions, and eventually death if not treated
handrail	a physical feature that runs parallel to the desired route which is used as a guide

hypothermia	see 'exposure'
insulation layer	the layer of clothing worn over the base layer, and which protects the body from the effects of heat loss by acting as a barrier
shell layer	the outer layer of clothing, which protects the insulation layer from the adverse affects of wind and water
tick off features	features on the ground which can be noted and mentally 'ticked-of'' as they are passed, and then compared with progress on the map
thumbing	using the thumb like a bookmark to indicate the last position or tick off feature passed on the map; the map is usually folded to make this easier
trig point	a triangulation point, formerly used by surveyors of the Ordnance Survey to determine the height and position of peaks; this is now done by aerial photography; trig points are usually marked by concrete columns
wicking	the process by which moisture is transmitted from the skin to the outer layers of clothing

INDEX OF PLACE NAMES

3 Peaks
Bunkroom 88

B
Bainbridge 17
Beecroft Hall 69, 80
Birkwith Cave 57, 76
Blea Moor 10, 43, 63
Blindbeck 88
Brackenbottom 7, 38, 53, 71, 78
Braithwaite Wife Hole 15, 16, 48, 65, 78
Broadrake 46
Brow Gill Beck 58

C
Carlisle 18, 37, 59
Chapel le Dale 6, 19, 20, 29, 47, 88, 89
Clapham 67
Colt Park 51
Cragg Hill Farm 88
Crown Hotel 41, 69, 80, 88

D
Deepdale 44
Dent Head 43
Dentdale 43, 46

F
Force Gill 43

G
Gaping Gill 15
Giggleswick 16
God's Bridge 58, 76
Golden Lion 38, 41, 53, 69, 71, 88
Great Douk Cave 9, 47, 51
Greensett Tarn 44
Gunnerfleet Farm 46, 60, 65, 76

H
Hawes 37, 42, 59, 62, 78
Hill Inn 3, 6, 7, 10, 15, 16, 29, 30, 47, 50-52, 59, 62, 64, 70, 78, 84, 86, 87, 89
Holme Farm 88
Horton in Ribblesdale 3, 6, 7, 11, 29, 37, 41, 50, 52, 53, 64, 66-68, 70, 71, 79, 80, 85-88, 90
Horton Lane 11, 55, 74
Horton Quarry 69, 80
Horton Railway Station 69, 80
Hull Pot 10, 40, 55, 74
Humphrey Bottom 49

I
Ingleborough 4, 7, 9, 12-17, 20, 37, 44, 47, 50, 52, 64, 67, 77-79, 84, 86
Ingleborough National Nature Reserve 16
Ingleton 17, 37, 42, 43, 46, 59, 62, 65, 78, 89-91
Ireby 17
Ivescar Farm 46

L
Ling Gill Beck 58, 76
Lodge Hall 58, 76

N
Nether Lodge 58, 76

P
Park Fell 47, 50, 66, 79
Pen y Ghent 3, 6, 7, 10, 11, 13-15, 17, 36, 37, 40, 47, 50, 52, 53, 67, 71, 79, 86, 87
Pen y Ghent Café 29, 30, 38, 41, 53, 69, 71, 80, 88, 90, 91
Pennine Way 39, 40, 54-56, 71, 74, 76
Philpin Farm 62, 78

R
Red Moss 7, 57
Ribblehead 3, 6, 8, 10-12, 17, 20, 29, 30, 42, 43, 45, 52, 53, 58, 59, 63-65, 70, 76, 86-89
Ribblehead Viaduct 10, 19, 42, 46, 50, 60, 63, 76

S
Sell Gill Beck 56, 75
Sell Gill Holes 11
Settle 16, 18, 37, 42, 59, 71, 89-91
Simon Fell 47, 50
Southerscales 7
Southerscales Nature Reserve 16, 48, 65, 78
St Oswald (church) 38, 53, 71
Station Inn 10, 42, 46, 58, 59, 63, 64, 76, 89
Sulber 8, 68, 80
Sulber Nick 7

T
The Crown Hotel 41, 69, 80, 88
The Golden Lion 38, 41, 53, 69, 71, 88
The Hill Inn 3, 6, 7, 10, 15, 29, 30, 47, 50-52, 59, 62, 64, 70, 78, 84, 86, 87, 89
The Knoll 88
The Old School Bunkhouse 89
The Pennine Way 39, 40, 54-56
The Station Inn 10, 42, 46, 58, 59, 63, 64, 76, 89
Three Peaks Club 13, 29, 91
Todber Moss 7, 10, 11, 57
Townhead 90

W
Whernside 3, 7, 8, 13, 14, 37, 42, 45, 47, 50, 52, 58, 63, 73, 77, 86, 87
Winterscales Beck 60, 76
Winterscales Farm 7, 59, 60, 76

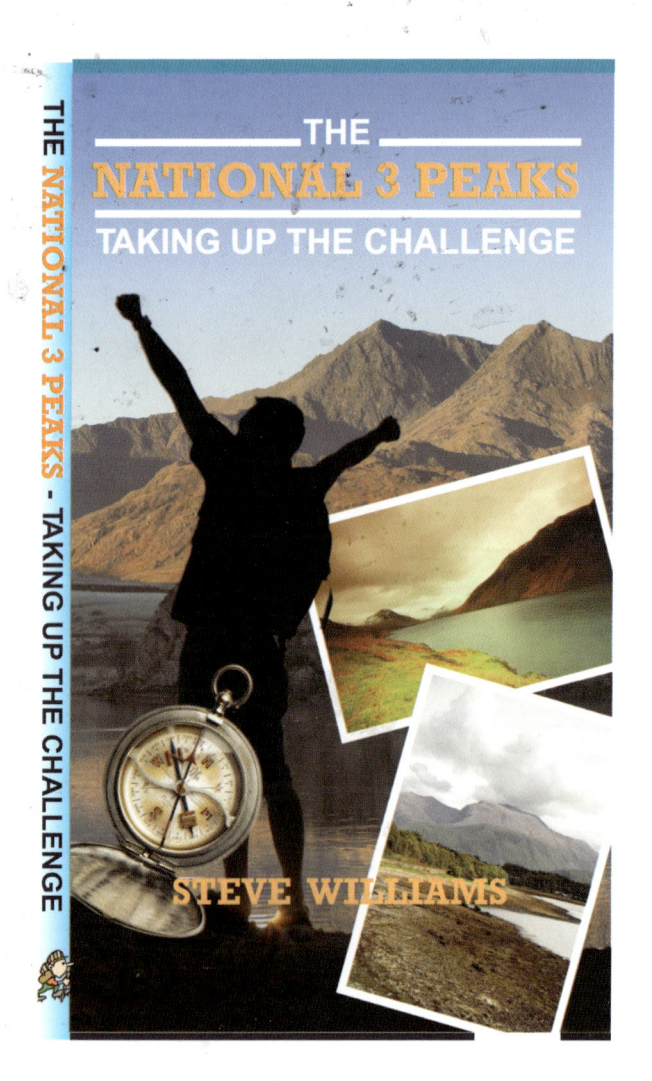

If you've enjoyed **The Yorkshire Three Peaks Challenge** then why not consider tackling **The National Three Peaks Challenge**?

The National 3 Peaks - Taking Up The Challenge
with
Steve Williams

Published by Discovery Walking Guides Ltd.
ISBN 9781904946915
£8.99